The Potter
and the
Clay

The Potter and the Clay

Meditations on Spiritual Growth

Thomas R. Hawkins

The Upper Room
Nashville, Tennessee

Scripture quotations not otherwise identified are from the Revised
Standard Version of the Bible, copyrighted 1946, 1952, and © 1971
by the Division of Christian Education, National Council of the
Churches of Christ in the United States of America, and are used
by permission.

Scripture quotations designated NEB are from *The New English
Bible*, © The Delegates of the Oxford University Press and the
Syndics of Cambridge University Press 1961 and 1970, and are
reprinted by permission.

Scripture quotations designated JB are from *The Jerusalem Bible*,
copyright © 1966 by Darton, Longman & Todd, Ltd. and Double-
day & Company, Inc. Used by permission of the publisher.

Scripture quotations designated NIV are from the *Holy Bible: New
International Version*. Copyright © 1978 by the New York Interna-
tional Bible Society. Used by permission of Zondervan Bible Pub-
lishers.

Excerpts from *The Firstborn* by Christopher Fry, published by Ox-
ford University Press, are used by permission of the publisher.

Excerpts from "In Time of 'The Breaking of Nations'" from THE
COMPLETE POEMS OF THOMAS HARDY edited by James Gib-
son. Published by Macmillan Publishing Company, 1978. Used by
permission of Macmillan Publishing Company (New York) and
Macmillan (London) Ltd.

Excerpts from "Little Gidding" and "The Dry Salvages" in FOUR
QUARTETS, copyright 1943 by T.S. Eliot; renewed 1971 by Esme
Valerie Eliot. Reprinted by permission of Harcourt Brace
Jovanovich, Inc. and Faber & Faber, London.

Book Design: J. S. Laughbaum
First Printing: March 1986 (5)
Library of Congress Catalog Card Number: 85-52018
ISBN 0-8358-0537-9

Printed in the United States of America

In memory of
Robert Sherman Hawkins
and
William Sherman Hawkins

Contents

Introduction

I attended an open-country church in east central Illinois as a young adult. The church possessed only a limited repertoire of hymns and songs. One of the most familiar selections was "Have Thine Own Way, Lord" by Adelaide A. Pollard:

> Have thine own way, Lord!
> Have thine own way!
> Thou art the potter;
> I am the clay.
>
> Mold me and make me
> After thy will,
> While I am waiting,
> Yielded and still.[1]

Potters and clay are ever-present images in our storehouse of religious metaphors. We sing about them. We hear sermons with illustrations drawn from them. We refer to them in our discussions and Bible study.

In spite of our fondness for potters and clay, few of us have ever plunged our hands into the actual craft. We seldom have any firsthand experience with clay. Even the most passing acquaintance with what real potters do with real clay lies beyond our experience.

My own exposure to pottery was similarly limited until recently. My eighth-grade art teacher did try to help us know the various art media. We gathered sycamore leaves one fall day and pressed them into moist clay. Later, we trimmed the edges and bent them slightly, forming an ash tray. They were then kiln-fired and glazed. Mine was a faded turquoise lump. I gave it to my father for Christmas. He knocked the ashes from his pipe into it one evening and—whether by accident or not, I don't know—shattered it into a dozen pieces.

A few years ago, I decided that I needed to break my workaholic patterns. I thought that I might reactivate my childhood collections of coins and stamps. I tried jogging and tennis. One was too sedentary; the other, too exhausting. My eyes fell upon the course announcements of a local community college one evening. I noticed a course on beginning pottery. The next week, I was in mud up to my elbows.

I spent the next months compulsively wedging clay and throwing pots. I was so absorbed in mastering the potter's technical skills that I seldom reflected upon the meaning of my actions. Gradually I began to grasp why pottery had always fascinated biblical prophets and Christian preachers. I understood why those interested in formation and transformation had found in pottery a powerful metaphor.

Although I had sought pottery as an escape from my work, I began to realize that there were many inescapable connections between the two. The following meditations are the fruit of that realization. They have two primary aims. First, since pottery images are so prevalent in Christian discourse, they seek to provide some basic, practical information about what a potter actually does with the clay. This should help the average Christian—both laypersons and clergy—to understand more fully the images they so freely use and abuse. Second, these meditations have allowed me to share the insights that came to me as I plunged my own hands into clay. Christian formation, particularly the roles of imagination and of obedience in the transformative process, was a major preoccupation while I was actively working with clay. My meditations reflect these concerns. Many people are struggling to understand what all the talk about Christian formation means. To discuss this novel and slightly unfamiliar topic through the lens of "the potter and the clay" may enable those who are unacquainted with Christian formation to understand some aspects of it.

These meditations follow the ceramic process from the gathering of the raw materials to the evaluation of the finished product. Their development, consequently, is linear. They move from stage one to stage eight, from beginning to end. The ideas and images that are explored, on the other hand, follow a cyclic evolution. Certain themes and concerns recur at various stages of the pot's transformation. Just because chapter 1 presents a certain theme while discussing the assembling of raw materials does not mean that the same theme will not recur when the firing process is explored. The various phases of the ceramic process serve as different angles that illuminate unsuspected facets of one diamond.

This diamond is a living vessel: the person. Within this earthen vessel, states Paul, is a treasure (2 Cor. 4:7). The task of Christian transformation can be likened both to the treasure passively uncovered in a field and to the one actively sought.

The kingdom of heaven is like treasure hidden in a field, which a man found and covered up; then in his joy he goes and sells all that he has and buys that field. Again, the kingdom of heaven is like a merchant in search of fine pearls, who, on finding one pearl of great value, went and sold all that he had and bought it.

—Matthew 13:44-46

We must work out our salvation with fear and trembling. We must also rely totally upon God's grace at work within us. At the heart of Christian transformation is a dynamic interaction between action and rest, doing and being, trusting oneself and trusting forces beyond oneself.

The potter and the clay are involved in this same creative process. The potter must rely on his own abilities; but he must trust his creations to processes beyond his control. The potter must know when to mold the clay with her hands and when to release it. The clay both responds to the potter and also resists. It is simultaneously free and limited. This same paradox lies at the heart of Christian experience. To do pottery is to reflect upon these mysterious ways that God uses to shape our lives. To do pottery is to come to a fuller understanding of what growth toward maturity entails.

Gathering
The Raw Materials

I have no idea why I saved it all those years. There it was, nestled among the tissue and newsprint in the bottom of a box marked "desk drawers, upstairs." It had lain there silently waiting all these years, packed away in a dark corner of the attic. I brushed the yellowed newsprint aside and held it in my hand. Closing my eyes, I tried to remember where it came from and why I had valued it enough to put it in my desk drawer.

No answer came. For some long-forgotten reason my eyes and hands had been attracted to this worn chunk of granite. Crystalline bits of quartz, orthoclase, and mica sparkled from deep within the dark, grey stone. Perhaps I had collected it sometime during junior high school. Our science teacher, in the vain attempt to teach us something about our world, had required us to assemble collections of leaves, insects, and other natural objects. All one hundred sheets of my leaf collection, which I had carefully pressed, dried, and mounted, still stand at the back of a filing cabinet drawer. Is this stone a first cousin to those brittle and faded leaves? Perhaps I had brought it home from my grandparents' front porch. It was an open porch with a green wooden swing and a

13

cushioned glider that faced the street. The floor and the low, red-brick walls were littered with arrowheads, stone axes, stalactites, stalagmites, desert roses of sandstone, and other oddities that they had accumulated. More probably I had found it embedded in the clay streamed that ran through our pasture. I had once loved to wade and to dig there during hot summer afternoons while the Jerseys and Holsteins slept under enormous, ancient oaks that lined the waterway.

The persistent action of water had worn the stone's surface to a smooth and delicate finish. The rough, coarse texture of the granite had been ground to a dull but pleasing patina. I rub my fingers over the stone and feel its coolness. My thumb slips into a small depression that has eroded away along one side. Constant abrasion and friction have left their imprint upon this stone. What was once a jagged and sharp projectile torn from the inner earth is now a smooth, elliptical stone egg.

I feel this time-worn egg and remember. I remember a time before the contents of my childhood bedroom were packed and scattered to a dozen different houses. The pasture. The milk cows under the massive oaks. The buzzing of insects. The swish, swish of tails. The bubbling of water as its liquid, unvarying current shatters on stones only to come up full of air and foam. The faded red barn. The sagging wire fence propped up with osage orange posts. A thousand different colors of green flash in the sunlight.

I am not the only one who remembers. The planet itself remembers through this same stone. It remembers not my own personal history or even human history but rather earth history. Long ago, so long ago that time loses all meaning, the crust of the earth heaves and buckles. Volcanoes belch boiling clouds of steam and dust. Glowing liquid stone bubbles and oozes forth. Fiery fountains and geysers dance on lakes of molten lava. A blazing sea of stone from deep within the earth spreads across the landscape. Slowly the fiery red stone cools and turns glossy black, pitted with acid potmarks. The billowing clouds of steam that have risen from the volcanic magmas condense into rain and fall, only to explode once more into gas and steam as they touch the surface of the still burning stone.

At last there comes a time when the rocks are no longer so hot. The raindrops no longer recoil from the stone, hissing and boiling. The rain puddles up into basins. The water first trickles and then pours down the steep mountains. Erosion begins to wear away the barren, sterile stone slopes.

Earthquakes convulse the newly formed crust. Stone ledges twist and rise into high cliffs. Fault lines between the tectonic plates shift as more hot lava rises and spills over the land. While these dramatic and cataclysmic transformations shake the earthscape, the rain and water go on with their patient, silent sculpting of the land.

Grey-green lichens evolve and eat away the pot-marked stone. Wind and water erode tiny particles and carry them into streams and rivers. These deposits make their way back into the depths of the earth, only to be pressed by the planet's tremendous heat and weight back into stone once again. These new formations then make their way back to the crust where they are fragmented and worn down once again.

I hold eternity in my hand. Gazing into this worn, granite egg, I peer into the timeless cycles of our planet's birth, decay, and rebirth. The mica and quartz embedded within the grey stone witness to countless cycles of fragmentation and fusion, of breaking and mending. It is a process that is so slow, so ubiquitous, that we are hardly aware of it.

Outside my window is a little whirlwind of dust blowing between the cobblestones and skittering down the street. The wind amuses itself with these tiny grains of our planet that once were as solid as my childhood stone egg, dug from among the decaying leaves at the bottom of the pasture stream. Rocks that have been ground to powder by the constant action of wind and rain are everywhere: under our feet, beneath our wheels, in the air. The clouds of dust kicked up by our feet in the garden or by the wind along the street are as ephemeral as the wispy cloud that the breeze pushes across the sky, only to break apart just beyond the horizon. Yet once this dry powder was liquid fire, bubbling and dancing in the lava flow. Once this dust was a jagged piece of stone capable of cutting our feet should we have stepped upon it. Made of decomposed stone that has abandoned its crystalline palace, this dust enters our rivers and streams on its uncertain journey to the bottom of lakes and oceans. Eons of hydrothermal activity or the weight of subsequent deposits will transform it back into stone; and then the slow process of decay begins again. These geologic processes are cyclic: stone to dust to stone to dust to stone.

I place the long-lost stone atop a precariously balanced pile of papers, beside the cup of coffee that I am drinking. Until just a few months ago, this cup was nothing more than a lump of wet clay. It was a mass of decomposed stone particles that were held together by water and their mutual attraction. I shaped it on a potter's wheel, glazed it, fired it, created it. The stone and the cup are both products of transformation. Both are made of the provisional, ephemeral stuff of the earth. Both have submitted to dramatic processes of transmutation.

The potter's ceramic techniques reproduce in some measure the natural geologic processes of our planet. Like the earth itself, the potter uses pressure and fire to convert pulverized rock back into stone. Something fleeting and plastic is given a definitive shape and form. The potter's fiery kiln replicates the volcano's blazing heat. The combination of the wheel's centrifugal force and of the human hand's steady pressure achieves a result that is not unlike that of the earth's own hydrothermal compaction.

There is, however, a significant difference in the time taken by these two processes. The potter does in a matter of days what nature accomplishes over vast millenia. The crushed stone in our driveways erodes and decays so slowly that we cannot see it happening. A few molecules are attracted to other elements and pull away from the stone. The action of the rain and sun wear away the stone's surface. Yet even if we were to look at it carefully every day over a whole lifetime, we would hardly be aware of any change. Everything changes. Everything moves. Our eyes, however, cannot always perceive it. Our lives are too short to comprehend it. Our seeing is not only limited by our lifespan; it is also circumscribed by our eyes. The physical structure of our eyes has a critical fusion frequency that enables us to see only events that happen no faster than fifty times a second. Motion picture still frames, for example, move at a rate of only twenty-four frames per second. Thus, we cannot see the frantic movements of atoms and molecules that constantly rearrange the invisible structure of the stone. Nor can we perceive the other vaster and more timeless processes of erosion. Nature's persistent abrasion grinds down the stone's bodily surface. Yet

17

many lifetimes must pass before the human eye can detect it.

The potter's processes, on the other hand, occur on a more human scale. We can see, touch, witness the changes that the potter effects. The clay that is formless and boundless today may be wedged, thrown, and fired tomorrow. Within the course of a few days the clay may lose its plastic character and be given an ultimate and eternal configuration. The potter harnesses and uses for his own purposes the natural forces that cause the stone either to break apart or to fuse together into new stone. The potter's intervention accelerates these forces in order to generate a purely human creation.

The potter imposes upon the formless cycles of natural decay and generation some order and limitation. This manipulation of geologic change has one important effect: it brings to a definitive conclusion the cycles of natural transformation. Through his intervention, the potter disrupts the cyclic geologic evolution. He introduces a ceramic evolution that is a linear, goal-oriented alteration. This more strictly human action breaks nature's patient rhythm of recapitulation and eternal return. Once transformed in the potter's furnace, the clay vessel may break or shatter; but it never again will be eroded by wind and water. The potsherds are indestructible. The potter assembles nature's own provisional materials and through an irreversible transmutation destines them to become a new, unchanging reality.

This utter permanence of pottery is the main reason for its archeological value. Broken pottery is cast aside and left to accumulate. Layer over layer, settlement over settlement, piles up. Eventually the site is abandoned until the modern archeologist arrives. As an archeological excavation proceeds, broken pottery comes in daily by the basketful. Sometimes as many as fifty or a hundred baskets may be gathered in a single day. These are carefully recorded by layer and by stratum. Since each successive occupation layer has its own distinctive ceramics, the pottery provides a tool for dating and classifying the various occupation levels. Because it is indestructible, this dating is as secure as the sequence dating of fossils frozen in sedimentary rocks.

Among all the crafts learned by early humankind, pottery was the first to modify the physical realm and to give a quasi-permanence to human creations. The potter's dream is to transmute the incoherence of nature into order. She seeks to lead the plastic clay into a new state of fixity. The sculptor proceeds by subtraction of material from a mass of stone, liberating a static form. The painter works with liquid upon a surface plane to create an image that always remains something of an abstraction from reality rather than reality itself. The potter's objective is very different. The potter immerses herself in something as fluid and fleeting as moist clay in order to create a permanent reality. The potter must coordinate simultaneously matter, movement, and energy—those basic constituents of our ever-changing reality—in the attempt to produce something eternal and unchanging.

When and how this ceramic discovery was made is now lost amid the rubble of prehistoric civilization. The invention of pottery lagged behind many other technological developments of Neolithic culture. Stone Age people knew how to work with stone and bone, to weave baskets, and to work leather. Pottery, on the other hand, was discovered much later. This slow development is probably related to the nomadic character of Neolithic life. Only when bands and · families settled down into agricultural communities could cheap and easily broken ceramic ware take its place alongside unbreakable materials such as bone, stone, or shells.[1]

Excavations of Neolithic sites at biblical Jericho and in the Kurdish foothills suggest that people learned about firing clay entirely by accident. Homes had shallow pits in the floor that were probably used for cooking. Families began to coat these pits with clay. The cooking fire then hardened the clay into a fixed basin. Neolithic households eventually realized the value of these watertight clay vessels and began to make them separately. Other archeologists suggest that the clay was first used to seal reed baskets. One such clay-coated basket accidentally fell into a fire. The reed and fiber burned away, but the clay hardened into a vessel. An accident of this sort then triggered the discovery that clay could be fired into permanent, watertight receptacles.[2]

Whatever the means by which early men and women discovered the ceramic process, they soon found that it could supply them with something more than just watertight vessels in which to store food. Like the carefully chipped flint arrowhead and the cave paintings of Lausanne, pottery could give an outward, artistic expression to inner visions. At the beginning of all created things there is the idea. The word *idea* comes from the Greek word *eidos*, which means something you reach with your eyes, something seen by the mind. An idea is a form you see with the inner eye. The potter discovered that the shape or form imagined by the inner eye could be imposed on matter and then fired into the lasting permanence of stone. The potter discovered that she could influence reality through her own personal imagination and awareness. Nature may be the place of inspiration and the source of the materials for the ceramic process, but the potter accomplishes something other than what nature can effect. The potter intervenes at the heart of matter to give it another shape that she has dreamed and imagined, that she has seen with an inner eye. The form is built upon the potter's wheel in a complex dialogue among the hands, the clay, and the imagination. Something unique, personal, and human is given lasting shape amid the boundless, formless world of nature's cycles.

The potter always works toward the goal of impressing this inner, fixed form upon the changing, ill-defined world about her. A potter's creations always reflect her own body and spirit. A woman with small and delicate hands cannot easily throw large and bulky pots. A man who is always in a hurry and careless about what he does will create pots that look rushed and careless. Someone who is trained in ceramics has only to glance at a pot in order to determine whether it is the work of Peter Volkos or Mary Rogers. A potter's distinctive inner vision is revealed in every pot that he produces. The same is true of the pottery produced by whole cultures. Each culture and historical period have their own distinctive inner construct. The red and black painted ware of classical Greece is easily distinguished from the Khirbet Kerak ware produced near the Sea of Galilee during the early Bronze Age.

Look at the spout on your milk pitcher. Only a human hand could have invented such a shape. It is no natural form. Water wearing away the stone would never produce this combination of curves and lines. The contours of the human hand alone determine these outlines. The single finger of one hand presses the thin wall of moist clay between the outspread fingers of the second hand. Long before it was molded by a human hand, however, this pouring spout was

21

conceived within the human imagination. The potter, as a representative of human culture, locates us in time and space by fixing into permanent forms our inner, imaginative constructs. Amid all the rhythms of nature, this form, this idea made flesh, endures. The potter uses the measured cadences of nature, but she sets them to a different musical score.

Pottery tells us something about the obscure natural energies beyond our control. It takes natural forces that operate in geological change and speeds them up. Changes that would take millenia to happen occur in a matter of days, allowing us to witness transformations that otherwise would remain beyond us. Pottery reveals how the human subject is not just a powerless monad carried along by majestic but indifferent forces. It discloses something fundamental about our capacity to give both form and permanence to some aspects of our lives in spite of those natural cycles that sweep us away towards death. The potter utilizes natural processes, but he alters their character within certain fixed limits. Out of the flux of geologic change, something is given lasting value because it was touched by the human hand. It rises above the blind cycles of nature and attains a new level of reality. What was formerly a vast and awful cosmos that was indifferent to human feeling and spirit now acquires the imprint of the human touch and is given a human face. This is pottery's revelatory capacity.

For these reasons pottery has always attracted the attention of those poets and prophets who were interested in the mechanics of human transformation. We are all the products of transformation. Like the coffee cup and the worn stone egg, I am not the same person that I was when I stood in the sunlit pasture. I am not even the same person who sat last week at the kickwheel and turned a ginger jar. Wave after wave of change has swept over me and will continue to work its effects within me. Many of these processes differ little from the cyclic energies of geologic fragmentation and formation that create both the feldspar and the clay. Both the lump of basalt and the tiny baby are embedded in the same formless, boundless cyclic world of nature.

We are hardly aware of the continuous changes at work within our bodies. Every seven years all the cells of our bodies (with the exception of a woman's ova and some human brain cells) die, are exhaled, are washed off, or fall away. We grow new skin cells every day. With the blink of our eyes we flush cells down our tear ducts. The entire lining of our mouth is washed away and digested with every meal. We lose about a soup plate full of cells every day. Every one of these cells must somehow be replaced.[3]

Within our bodies is a cellular upheaval that is not unlike the cataclysmic convulsions of our planet. Within us there is a constant fragmentation and fusion, decay and recreation, erosion and regeneration. All this happens so silently, so constantly, that we never sense it. Our lives are dependent upon the smooth functioning of these strange and obscure processes. Without them we would perish.

> At the interior of our cells, driving them, providing the oxidative energy that sends us out for the improvement of each shining day, are the mitochondria, and in a strict sense they are not ours. They turn out to be little separate creatures, the colonial posterity of migrant prokaryocytes, probably primitive bacteria that swam into ancestral precursors of our eukaryotic cells and stayed there . . . . they have maintained themselves and their ways, replicating in their own

fashion, privately, with their own DNA and RNA quite different from ours . . . without them, we would not move a muscle, drum a finger, think a thought.[4]

Our lives arise out of these interconnections and energies that remain always a mystery to us and over which we exercise almost no control. Chromosomes randomly fuse and determine our sexual gender. Slender threads of DNA separate, mingle, and recombine. The capacity to blunder slightly, to create something totally spontaneous and unpredictable, is the real marvel of DNA and accounts for the surprising variety and adaptability of our species.[5] These forces determine our gender, our innate tendencies toward certain diseases, the color of our hair, and perhaps even our dispositions.

Even as the mica or basalt have little control over the forces that first grind them into dust and then fuse them into new stones, so we have little control over vast living processes that shape our lives. There is something frightening in this realization. It can leave us feeling terribly vulnerable in an empty, vast universe:

> When I look at thy heavens, the work of thy fingers,
>> the moon and the stars which thou hast
>> established;
> what is man that thou art mindful of him,
>> and the son of man that thou dost care for him?
>> —Psalm 8:3-4

Our wonder at the complexity and mystery of life is mingled with both awe and terror.

Our terrible feeling of powerlessness, however, is balanced against our very real capacity to shape this awesome universe. The psalmist's sense of awe is balanced with a sense of healthy self-confidence. This natural reality is not blind and indifferent. We can adduce a divine purpose, an inner "idea" from the mind of God, that seeks to shape our world. Our own capacity to shape and create allows us to infer that there is a cosmic Creator with whom we are co-creators:

> Yet thou hast made him little less than God,
>   and dost crown him with glory and honor.
> Thou hast given him dominion
>   over the works of thy hands;
>   thou hast put all things under his feet.
> . . . .
> O Lord, our Lord,
>   how majestic is thy name in all the earth!
> —Psalm 8:5-6, 9

Elsewhere in nature, these energies and cycles are automatic. The tadpole changes into a frog. The caterpillar has no choice about spinning its cocoon and becoming a butterfly. We speak of wanting to live "as free as a bird." Yet a bird's life is rigidly controlled and determined. Instinctual patterns govern its whole life cycle. We are the only creatures that rise above the rigid determinism of nature. There is an element of self-direction in our lives. We are capable of shaping some dimensions of our personal reality. Our actions can attain some lasting, unchanging shape. Central to this task of self-direction is our capacity to imagine. We can generate within ourselves models, paradigms, and mental constructs that are then tested against and implemented in our material, exterior world.

This whole process of transcending the natural cycles and attaining some measure of self-direction in our lives is also the potter's task. As pottery is to the natural geologic process, so our self-direction is to our human development and transformation. Our ideas—

what we "see" with our interior eyes—become the inner center from which we seek to coordinate the ever-shifting fragments of our experience into some meaningful whole. This whole, we hope, may acquire some lasting, permanent character. We seek some active mastery over the vicissitudes of outer experience and inner impulse, an abiding sense of inner centeredness.

Human transformation is not just a matter of passive unfolding. It is a complicated synthesis of activity and passivity. We regulate our lives through this constant dialogue between what we ourselves can do in our lives and those deeper ordering processes that come forth from beyond us. Our personal identity is this ability to combine the resiliency of essential patterns and imaginative possibilities within cycles of change that we cannot control. Erik Erikson states that human virtue is the strength to balance these passive and active elements in our lives:

> *Patiens*, then would denote a state of being exposed from within or from without to superior forces which cannot be overcome without prolonged patience or energetic and redeeming help; while *agens* connotes an inner state of being unbroken in initiative and of acting in the service of a cause which sanctions this initiative.[6]

There are vast currents in our lives that flow almost unbroken by our presence. Moving toward their own conclusion, they remain beyond our grasp and influence. Yet it is also necessary for us to shape our own identity. We regulate our lives through a constant dialogue between what we personally must do and what we must accept as coming to us from beyond.

The potter engages in this same task at a geologic rather than biologic and human level. The potter must achieve some synthesis between the active and passive dimensions. She seeks to harness the cyclic geologic processes and to cooperate with the energies of nature that always remain slightly beyond her complete control. She intervenes at the very heart of matter in order to give the clay another shape than the one that nature has given it. This new shape is one which she has dreamed and constructed in her imagination. From the center of her own being comes forth a vision, a possibility. This gestalt is then fixed by the totality of her gestures into something permanent. The potter imposes upon the limitless geologic cycles a permanent shape created according to her inner vision. This idea, this *eidos*, arises from some center deep within her. It is an "in-sight," a seeing from the interior center.

Each of us must do the same thing as the potter. We intervene at the heart of the biologic cycle to create a personal identity. Our transformations are not automatic. We must shape them ourselves. Possible models and paradigms for our lives arise from some inner center. Our insights direct us in the building of our personal realities. Our lives are built up like the moist clay as it is shaped in the potter's hands. They are not thrown up from the depths by volcanic and cyclic forces. Our lives are shaped by our visions and desires.

Yet our situation is still more complicated. We must choose to see this inner vision. We must choose to implement it rather than to allow ourselves to drift along the aimless stream of life. Living in obedience to this center and its insights, we impose certain boundaries upon reality and may attain something permanent and eternal in our lives. When we choose to ignore this center, then we lapse into a formless life without direction and purpose. Without any clear creative idea as to what he intends to make, even the best potter will produce only flat, truncated pots.

This marked similarity between the potter's role in shaping material reality and the individual's role in shaping a personal identity accounts for the importance of the ceramic motif in both Hebrew and Christian literature. Pottery becomes a symbol both for personal transformation and for cosmic transfiguration.

God operates in precisely the same manner as the potter. God speaks a word and brings form out of the void. In the beginning there was nothing but formless waste. God's spirit hovered over this boundless, plastic void and drew forth order from chaos. In the beginning God said, "Let there be light." The Hebrew word for "to speak," *dabar,* is notoriously difficult to translate. It means not just speech but event, thought, affair. The spoken word arises out of an inner disposition. This inner disposition has the capacity to change reality.

> For as the heavens are higher than the earth,
> so are my ways higher than your ways
>   and my thoughts than your thoughts;
> and as the rain and the snow come down from heaven
> and do not return until they have watered the earth,
>   making it blossom and bear fruit,
> and give seed for sowing and bread to eat,
> so shall the word which comes from my mouth
>   prevail;
>   it shall not return to me fruitless
> without accomplishing my purpose
>   or succeeding in the task I gave it.
>   —Isaiah 55:9-11, NEB

John's Gospel makes this point even more explicitly. Jesus Christ is the Word that was present in creation.

Jesus is the Word that God spoke when form was brought forth from the void. Because everything is alive with Christ's life, Christ is the inner center that holds all things together.

> In the beginning was the Word, and the Word was with God, and the Word was God. He was in the beginning with God; all things were made through him, and without him was not anything made that was made.
>
> —John 1:1-3

God becomes both the cosmic center from which all reality derives its being and also the inner center within each person. God becomes the potter who scoops the clay from the riverbank to shape a human person as well as the deeply interior center from which our insights and envisioned possibilities emerge.

The Christian affirmation is that we were meant to live in obedience to this center; but we have rejected this possibility and turned away from it. The neuroses and problems of human existence arise from the fact that we have replaced the images and life possibilities given to us by God with our own possibilities and fragmented visions. We ate the fruit of the tree of knowledge. We want to know our own possibilities and are not content to live with those God gives to us. Human development was meant to be life growing outward from this God-given center. But we have distorted this divine initiative by trying to live at our own center, out of our own knowledge and possibilities.

The goal of Christian transformation is to restore that imagining, creative center from which God can bring form to the chaos of our lives. In Jesus Christ we see the image and inner shape to which we are meant to conform. Human development is about the choice of which inner constructs we will allow to shape us. It is about our willingness to commit ourselves obediently to these constructs. Christian transformation is more specifically about the choice of Jesus Christ as this inner construct and about our willingness to undertake the painful process of conformity to his cross and resurrection.

To do pottery is often to touch with our hands and to sense in our hearts those vast waves of creation that flow through us and that shape our lives beneath our conscious experiencing. It allows us to reflect upon an inner process of which we are seldom aware. Pottery enables us to become attentive to those dynamics through which we both shape our lives and are shaped by them. It offers us an opportunity to come to a deeper awareness of the synthesis between human action and divine initiative that is called Christian transformation.

Wedging
The Raw Clay

I remove the plastic lid and drop it to the floor with a clatter. Reaching down into the barrel, I tear off a large, jagged chunk of clay from the reddish-brown mud. It feels hard, cold, and resistant. Its texture is stiff and cold. Replacing the lid on the barrel, I fling this recalcitrant hunk of clay down onto the plaster slab that serves as a wedging table. Rolling and twisting it as if it were a loaf of unbaked bread, I contend with the clay. I knead it with my palms. I throw my whole body into this action. It requires more than just my hands and arms. Soon my shoulders and back begin to ache. My muscles tighten and grow painful. Wedging the raw clay wears me down. This is perhaps the most critical step simply because it is the first one. If I do not wedge my clay properly, nothing else will happen correctly.

Two things take place as I apply pressure and gradually move toward the outside the clay particles that are deep inside the lump. First, air bubbles trapped inside the clay are broken open and exuded. Unless these are removed, the pot may be destroyed during the firing process. The sudden rise of temperature in the kiln may cause a trapped air bubble to explode, blowing a hole in the pot's wall. Since the clay must expand evenly during the building process and then contract uniformly during the firing, it is essential that the clay have some consistency. This is the second purpose of the wedging. All the minerals and other elements suspended in the raw clay are evenly distributed. Lumps and impurities are broken up and diffused throughout the whole ball of clay. The various subparticles are thus linked together and interconnected. Wedging rearranges and redistributes the clay particles. It assures the potter that the clay will have the consistency and interconnectedness that it needs to withstand expansion and contraction. It gives to the clay the extra tensile strength that it needs to survive the stresses of the ceramic process.

I press my palms deeply into the clay. It flattens and spreads under my pressure. I stand the heavy mass of clay on its end and, pressing down from the top, repeat the process. The clay on the outer edges is rolled into the center. Clay near the center is pressed down and outward toward the edges. The clay becomes something self-contained, whole. It is no longer just a small chunk torn away from a larger mass. Lumps and irregularities have been dissolved and their fragments distributed throughout the mass. The clay has achieved a certain homogeneity. Wedging forces the tiny clay platelets both to distribute themselves and to connect more fully with one another.

None of this is obvious to the human eye. The clay looks inert and solid. Beneath this surface appearance, however, is an intricate restructuring of clay platelets. The platelets interconnect; but it is not a rigid, static pattern. Each platelet is potentially connected to the next one. So there is an infinite number of ways in which the clay can structure itself. It must have some structure in order to exist. This structure, however, is never definitive or static. Our world is similar to this lump of clay. It is a consistent whole and not just some broken fragment. Everything is potentially connected to everything else. There is a given structure to reality, but it constantly rearranges itself. "I wonder whether you realize," wrote Baron von Hugel,

> a deep great fact? That souls—all human souls—are deeply interconnected? That, I mean, we can not only pray for each other, but suffer for each other . . . Nothing is more real than this interconnection—this gracious power put by God Himself into the very heart of our infirmities.[1]

This flowing interconnection is not just between one person and the next. It sparks and flashes between every God-created thing. Reality is not so much a set number of rigid, static "things" as it is an ever-shifting pattern of events.

The air that surrounds us is also within us. The fluid in our bodies is a perfect replica of that ancient sea in which we first came to life.[2] Looked at under an electron microscope, our skin appears more like the fjords of Norway or Maine's rocky coast than the solid, impermeable shell we perceive that it is. One function of our skin may not be to define us rigidly by keeping everything outside of us. It may create a ragged, spongelike surface where we can interact with our world. The biosphere is not just a hunk torn away from something else. It is consistent. There is a flow, a moving in and a moving out, between each living thing. Both the clay and the world seek strength through interconnectedness.

Some scientists hypothesize that the uniformity of all living things on earth arises from their ultimate derivation from some single cell that was fertilized by a lightning bolt as it floated in the Precambrian Sea.

From this parent cell all living things derive. One of our cells contains sufficient genetic information not only to reproduce us in our entirety but also to replicate every other living being. There is growing evidence that we still share our genes among one another. Genetic material may not be species-specific. The viruses,

> instead of being single-minded agents of disease and death, begin to look more like mobile genes . . . . We live in a dancing matrix of viruses; they dart, rather like bees, from organism to organism, from plant to insect to mammal to me and back again, and into the sea, tugging along pieces of this genome, strings of genes from that, transplanting grafts of DNA, passing around heredity as though at a great party.[3]

The rigid categories that we seek to establish between ourselves and the rest of the world may be an illusion.

The inner and outer realities may both flow into some greater unity that constitutes our real home. We are all interconnected: people whom we have never met and may never meet; animals we cannot imagine; glaciers and grains of sand and galaxies.

> They are each but cells of the one great body that, due to our present spiritual limitations, cannot keep conscious of its spatial boundaries. It forgets that since everything is joined to every other thing, one can escape the pain or the joy of another. But such spatial awareness, like the temporal awareness of our own ancestral unity, requires such intense comprehension that we can only hold it within us for a moment. And then it is gone. We are powerless to hold it any longer. Unable even to reconstruct it.[4]

Once, years ago, several members of my family were shingling my grandfather's barn roof. An approaching thunderstorm threatened us with its bolts of lightning, and we fled across the barn lot. A bolt struck the metal wire that my grandfather had stretched from the chicken house to a pole. This thin metal wire was enough to attract a flashing bolt of lightning. The charge leaped from the metal wire to one of our crew that happened to be walking quickly toward the house and paused briefly under the wire. The man's muscles twitched and shook uncontrollably for hours afterward. His heart raced and throbbed. The electric rhythms that pulse throughout the universe are the same whether they are pulsing in our hearts, driving our muscles, or cracking in the thunderstorm. There is a consistency in our world between our inmost heart and the sky above our heads.

If this is true of something so simple as electrical currents, why is it not true of our souls? John Climacus tells of a monk who was badly troubled by a demon. For twenty years he wore himself out with fasting and vigils, but the demon still harassed him. He wrote the temptation down on a small sheet of paper and went to a certain holy man. He gave the paper to him and, without saying a word, bowed to the ground. The old man read the paper, lifted the monk from the ground, and said to him, "My son, put your hand on my neck." The brother did this. "Very well," the holy man continued. "Now let this sin be on my neck for as many years as it has been or will be active within you. But from now on ignore it." Climacus assures his readers that this young monk was never again troubled by the demon.

The world, like the wedged clay, is a consistent, interconnected whole. All of us are potentially connected to everything else. We structure our life-world every moment by how we arrange these connections.

The number of possibilities is infinite and no definitive structure is possible. The poet John Donne wrote, "No man is an island, entire of itself; every man is a piece of the continent, a part of the main."[5] Gerard Manley Hopkins makes this same point in his poem, "Spring and Fall: to a young child." A young girl is troubled by the falling of the leaves. Hopkins intimates that she grieves because she senses the deep interconnections among all living things. Even the death of a leaf is as painful to her as her own death; and indeed it points to her own death:

> Margaret, are you grieving
> Over Goldengrove unleaving?
> Leaves, like the things of man, you
> With your fresh thoughts care for, can you?
> Ah! as the heart grows older
> It will come to such sights colder
> By and by, nor spare a sigh
> Though worlds of wanwood leafmeal lie;
> And yet you *will* weep and know why.
> Now no matter, child, the name:
> Sorrow's springs are the same.
> Nor mouth had, no nor mind, expressed
> What heart heard of, ghost guessed:
> It is the blight man was born for,
> It is Margaret you mourn for.[6]

The child's fresh eyes can perceive this interconnectedness. Sorrow's springs are the same in both leaf and person.

In Charles W. Williams' novel, *Descent into Hell*, Pauline is terrorized by her frequent visions of a poltergeist, a ghostlike double of herself. She confides her fears to Stanhope, one of the plot's male protagonists. Stanhope responds by asking Pauline why she has not asked a friend to carry her fear for her. He then offers to bear it on her behalf. The next time the apparition comes to frighten her, he explains, she will not need to be afraid. He will be carrying her fear for her. The only condition is that she must in turn agree to carry someone else's burden for them. Pauline regards this offer as sheer nonsense. Stanhope reminds her that bearing one another's burdens is very Christian and means decidedly more than listening sympathetically to someone else. It means accepting the fact that we are all interconnected and that we have an obligation to share someone else's pain.

> If you want to disobey and refuse the laws that are common to us all, if you want to live in pride and division and anger, you can. But if you will be part of the best of us, and live and laugh and be ashamed with us, then you must be content to be helped. You must give your burden up to someone else, and you must carry someone else's burden. I haven't made the universe and it isn't my fault. But I'm sure that this is a law of the universe, and not to give up your parcel is as much to rebel as not to carry another's.[7]

This interconnectedness, Williams intimates, is the central mystery of Christianity. It is the doctrine of substitution upon which we have staked our faith but which we have never completely understood. "There, rooted in the heart of the Church at its freshest, was the same strong thrust of interchange."[8]

Is not this notion of interchange at the heart of Christian prayer as well? When I truly pray for others, I take upon myself their burden. My energy flows into their situation. Their pain becomes my own. Perhaps this is why true prayer is so frightening and why we flee from it so quickly. When we pray we discover the deep-down interconnectedness of all things. Is this notion not at the heart of our understanding of Jesus' cross? Jesus bore our burdens for us on the cross. If our world is truly consistent and interconnected, then where and when this bearing of our burdens takes place is not really critical. The fact that Jesus died two thousand years ago no longer becomes a barrier to its immediacy for me in the here and now. Time and space curve in upon themselves until they meet. When the Hebrew Bible recites that a wandering Aramean was "my father" and when Jesus tells his disciples that he will be with them even unto the end of time, this is not just fanciful speculation or wishful thinking. They are profound and accurate statements about our world's interconnection and consistency.

As I continue to wedge the clay, I realize that there is another meaning to this interchange. I cut the clay with a wire. It slices through the soft lump and the two halves fall away from each other. I study the interior to look for irregularities that mar the clay's consistency. I cut it again and check for small pockets of trapped air. I dislike wedging the clay. Sometimes I delay working simply because I know that I must start with this. Isn't there a pot somewhere that I need to glaze? To trim? Wedging seems so slow and unproductive. I could build two or three vessels at the wheel in the time I spend wedging this one lump of unformed clay. Throwing the pots is definitely more exciting. But the wedging forces me to slow down and to focus upon the task at hand. I am forced to think about what I am feeling with my hands. This sense of the clay's feel in my hands is important. Much of a potter's work depends upon his knowledge of how the clay responds to his touch. I let my hands rest upon the clay.

It is now even and smooth. The clay is no longer cold and stiff. It moves and bends easily. I hold it in my hands and feel its warmth. Its resistance has been replaced by a warm obedience to my touch. I look at my hands that are caked with clay. The clay already has begun to dry and to harden around my fingernails. My hands feel dry. When I wash them at the end of the day, they will be chapped and cracked. My skin will drink up hand cream as quickly as I can rub it into my palms. The clay has drawn the moisture out of my own body, absorbing it into its own being. It has pulled the warmth of my own pumping, pulsing flesh into its cold, inert body. My warmth and my body fluids have brought the clay to life. It is only soft and pliable because it has partaken of my life.

The clay and my hands have engaged in an intricate dance. They have exchanged qualities and characteristics. My hands are stiff and aching, but the resistant clay is now easy to work. My fingers are dry, but the clay is soft. My shoulders and back throb with pain, but the once inert clay is now alive. When he plunges his hands into the clay, the potter experiences a temporary diminishment of his own vitality. He suffers this in order to bring something else to life. The thrill of creation will eventually restore the potter's diminished strength. My first teacher suffered from severe arthritis. Her hands could not easily stretch and bend. She had worked with the cold, damp clay during too many winters. Yet her love of creating new forms and images was unflagging. Through the created vessel, the potter will experience an ultimate expansion of being. Only this anticipated enjoyment renders the immediate suffering tolerable.

The Hebrew word *yotzer* can mean either "potter" or "creator." Genesis 2:19 portrays God as a divine potter at work on earthly clay. Our living, breathing world draws its life from the Creator's own hands. Is this molding and shaping as costly to God as it is to the potter? In giving our world life and being, does God undergo diminishment? Genesis implies that God was involved in our creation to a greater extent than in the creation of other living things. It took more than just a spoken word to call us into being. There was the vital exchange in which God's hands not only touched and molded the clay but also breathed upon it. The cold, inert clay became warm and alive. The process is described in terms that remind us of the typical potter at work on clay.

Creation is costly to God. God's constant infusion of life and of new possibilities into our world effects a diminishment within God's own being. Why then does God endure this diminishment? Why does God submit to something so costly as creation? As our own creation? James Weldon Johnson has captured the drama and power of creation in his poetry. He also suggests a possible answer to this question.

> And God stepped out on space,
> And he looked around and said:
> I'm lonely—
> I'll make me a world.
>
> And far as the eye of God could see
> Darkness covered everything,
> Blacker than a hundred midnights
> Down in a cypress swamp.
>
> Then God smiled,
> And the light broke,
> And the darkness rolled up on one side,
> And the light stood shining on the other,
> And God said: That's good!
>
> Then God reached out and took the light
>   in his hands,
> And God rolled the light around in his hands
> Until he made the sun.

. . . .

Then God walked around,
And God looked around
On all that he had made.
He looked at his sun;
And he looked at his moon,
And he looked at his little stars;
He looked on his world
With all its living things,
And God said: I'm lonely still.

Then God sat down—
On the side of a hill where he could think;
By a deep, wide river he sat down;
With his head in his hands,
God thought and thought,
Till he thought: I'll make me a man!

Up from the bed of the river
God scooped the clay;
And by the bank of the river
He kneeled him down;
And there the great God Almighty
Who lit the sun and fixed it in the sky,
Who flung the stars to the most far corner
   of the night,
Who rounded the earth in the middle of his hand;
This Great God,
Like a mammy bending over her baby,
Kneeled down in the dust
Toiling over a lump of clay
Till he shaped it in his own image;

Then into it he blew the breath of life,
And man became a living soul.
Amen. Amen.[9]

God spins out our cosmos from a desire to share the
divine life. God said, "I'm lonely!" God's single
intention in creation is to share life. In forming

41

humanity, God seeks to give a definitive shape to this yearning for intimacy. After Adam and Eve have eaten of the forbidden fruit, they hear God walking in the garden. Seeing themselves naked, they hide. God calls out, "Adam, where are you?" The only answer is the wind that rustles in the leaves and that kicks up tiny whirlwinds of dust. Where are you, Adam? Where are you, Eve? It is the plaintive cry of God's own loneliness.

There is an Hasidic tale of a rabbi's son who came home drenched with tears after playing a game of hide-and-seek. When the rabbi asked his son what had happened, the boy told his father that he had hidden but no one had bothered to seek him. The rabbi drew his son closer to him. You yourself now know how the Holy One of Israel feels, the rabbi said. God also hid from humankind in order to be sought. The Holy One still waits in vain for men and women to come and seek.[10]

God created the world out of this yearning for communion, this longing for intimacy. God has a hunger for experience. The divine consciousness flows through all things and wants to realize itself through intimacy. It rises unnamed through us. God is willing to take the risk of diminishment for the sake of this intensity of feeling. God accepts suffering in order to experience the satisfaction of creation. "The business of a supreme creative power is to set the stage," writes Charles Hartshorne, "for lesser types of creativity which the supreme creativity can take into its own endlessly enriched life."[11] The intricate dance between the clay and the potter's hands discloses that there is giving and receiving on both sides. Like a potter bending over the clay, God gives of the divine substance and energy in order to receive a new intensity of feeling.

The universe is a creation in the most complete sense of that word. It is something that has come forth from God, eternally bearing witness to its Creator. It is not some manufactured stuff. It is not an object to be dissected or a tool to be examined. The creation is an expression of being itself. It is more like a living being than like a digital wristwatch. When we look at the night sky, we are not looking at the strewn bits of some broken thing. We are looking at one vast expression of being, some immense interchange of life between it and its creator. Is this different from the vital and delicate exchange between the potter and the clay? Our living, breathing world draws its life from the creative hands that shape and form it.

God's constant infusion of life and of possibility into the world effects a diminishment within God's own being. This diminishment, however, is only temporary. The enjoyment and maximizing of new experience, which eventually flow back into God's life, compensate for this loss. God created humanity at great personal cost in order that it might give back to God the heightened awareness that arises from intimacy.

The Bible speaks of this giving and receiving through the metaphor of marriage. In love and intimacy there is a vital exchange. Each partner must experience diminishment in order to acquire an expansion of being. There is a profound paradox to this process whether we look at it from a human or cosmic level.

> Thus says the Lord,
> I remember the devotion of your youth,
>   your love as a bride,
> how you followed me in the wilderness,
>   in a land not sown.
>   —Jeremiah 2:2

It is a double tragedy when humankind, in which God has invested so much energy, resists God. When the created order receives from God but refuses to return the gift, then the very fabric of reality is rent asunder.

> Let me sing for my beloved
>   a love song concerning his vineyard:
> My beloved had a vineyard
>   on a very fertile hill.
> He digged it and cleared it of stones,
>   and planted it with choice vines;
> he built a watchtower in the midst of it,
>   and hewed out a wine vat in it;
> and he looked for it to yield grapes,
>   but it yielded wild grapes.
>   —Isaiah 5:1-2

God created the world out of a yearning for communion and intensity of feeling. Only this possibility made the diminishment of creation tolerable. This is why God has so consistently sought to restore the intimate relationship that once existed with both humankind and with the whole creation. God has a personal investment in creation that is akin to the potter's investment in the clay.

The suffering involved in creation already points to the cross. Even when humankind refuses to participate in the vital exchange of giving and receiving, God's investment is such that God cannot abandon the relationship.

> Is Ephraim still my dear son,
> a child in whom I delight?
>   As often as I turn my back on him
> I still remember him;
> and so my heart yearns for him,

I am filled with tenderness towards him.
This is the very word of the Lord.
—Jeremiah 31:20, NEB

God continually seeks the anticipated return of love. God still pursues the hope of realizing the divine consciousness in all things.

There is, therefore, a basic continuity to everything that God does. The cross is not some strange and unexpected act on God's part. It is not a last-ditch attempt to correct a sinful, fallen world. The cross must be seen as part of God's consistent attitude toward the world.

> The cross sheds a great deal of light on the intensity of God's desire to create the world. It illumines from within how strongly God wants human beings to be in communion with him. God redeems and reveals for the same reason that he creates.[12]

The cross is one more creative act. It seeks to establish the communion and intimacy that God intended in the very beginning. Like all of God's creative acts, it involves diminishment. God pours out the divine life and invests it in humankind, hoping that the flow of reciprocal love will be reestablished. The more divine energy that God is willing to risk, the greater the possibility that some creative, loving response will occur. There is one significant difference between the cross and the creation. On the cross God risks not just some divine warmth and breath. God risks the totality of Being. God in Christ,

> though he was in the form of God, did not count equality with God a thing to be grasped, but emptied himself, taking the form of a servant, being born in

45

the likeness of men. And being found in human form
he humbled himself and became obedient unto death,
even death on a cross.

—Philippians 2:6-8

God gambles that one final, ultimate act of self-
diminishment will restore communion between crea-
ture and Creator. This gamble was a success from the
Christian perspective. A new creation, responsive to
the molding touch of the divine potter, was established
in the midst of the world. Time and history are only
brief moments in God's measureless love. Cross and
creation remind us of God's constant pursuit of
intimacy with us. They also reveal the limitless risk
that God takes on our behalf.

Opening Up
The Center

Cupping the wedged clay between my hands, I lift it from the plaster slab. Gently I begin to shape it into a round snowball of mud. I thrust my thumbs into the center of this sphere. With my thumbs facing outward, I begin to pinch the walls of the clay upward. I rotate the ball in my hand. My hands must work quickly because the air will soon dry the clay and make it difficult to handle. If it becomes too dry, it will crack and split. Thick walls rise from the initial hole that I opened in the sphere's center. A small pot gradually takes shape. Walls rise and spread. The central opening grows wider and wider.

This is how the first Neolithic pots were probably made. Only later did the potter's kick wheel emerge. It also effected a cultural shift. Stone Age pottery was originally a woman's craft. The woman made pottery for cooking and for storage just as she performed the other household chores. In cultures where the kick wheel has not developed, pottery is still usually a woman's craft. With the development of the wheel came an industrialization of pottery. It became a profession. It also took more brute strength to maintain the speed and momentum of the wheel. Consequently, male potters replaced the women. A pot built by hand arises slowly from the initial opening up. Those built on the wheel are thrown more rapidly and require more complex combinations of the hands and feet. One element, however, remains stable in both techniques: one must begin from the center. The first stage is always the opening up of the clay's center.

I take another ball of wedged clay and place it firmly in the middle of a dry wheelhead. I begin kicking the lower flywheel with my right foot. The upper wheelhead gains speed. With the palm of my left hand I begin to direct steady pressure upon the mound of swiftly turning clay. The pad of my right hand rests above the mound, interlocked with the left hand, applying a downward pressure. The misshapen lump of clay begins to assume a definite form. The walls become straight. A slight dome, corresponding to the shape of my right hand, forms on top. I squeeze the clay upward between my two hands to create a cone. I tip the top of this cone over and downward, back into the mass of clay below. I repeat the process several times. Bringing the clay up, I then push it back down. The cone's spiral movement creates a similar spiraling within the clay platelets.

If we examined the clay under a microscope, we would see that it is made up of tiny ringlets or platelets. These platelets are twisted and scattered in every direction. They are interconnected, but the pattern is random. There is a structure, but it is not strong enough to withstand the ceramic process. I want to rearrange this pattern into something precise and strong. As I squeeze the clay into a spiral, these platelets gradually shift their positions. The scattered platelets begin to stack up one atop the next. These stacked platelets have much more tensile strength than the dispersed and loosely connected ones.

We would observe two things if we were to take two

sheets of perfectly polished glass, dampen them with water, and then apply them to one another. First, the two sheets would slide easily against one another. Second, they would be very difficult to pry apart. Suction produced by water would hold them together. The clay platelets behave in exactly the same way. The tightly stacked platelets give the clay added flexibility and extra strength. It needs these qualities to survive the pressures it will encounter. The clay acquires a perfect synthesis of resistance and suppleness, a marvelous equilibrium of forces that accept and refuse.

As it turns between my fingers, I begin to feel the clay moving into the center of the wheelhead. With the butt of my palm I create a small depression in the top of the clay. I hesitate, unsure whether the clay is truly on center. Taking a wooden needle, I kick the flywheel gently and let the clay turn slowly. My needle makes a thin mark on the outer edge of the clay. If it gouges deeply at one spot or does not touch the surface at another, I know the clay is not yet centered. I must repeat my spiraling movements until I have the clay on center. All this centering takes perhaps five minutes. It always looks easy. It even feels easy once it has been mastered. Beginners, however, often spend week after week trying to learn how to center the clay.

Centering is exceedingly difficult to do. For a long time I tried to apply too much pressure and to force the clay onto center. The results were frustrating. I threw the clay still further off center. Sometimes I even loosened it from the wheel and had to start over. Sometimes I removed my hands too quickly from the centered clay. My quick, jerky movements would throw it off center once more, and I would have to start over from the beginning. Centering is an act of bringing in, not of leaving out. It is effected not by force but by coordination. It is difficult, if not impossible, for a potter to force the clay onto center. The clay must move itself into the new shape.

Is this what it feels like to the Creator God who shapes both our lives and all creation? Is this what the Bible means when it speaks of our freedom? God does not impose the divine will upon us. God does not force us into any particular path. We are left with our freedom. Yet God's subtle pressure is always there. It is always resting upon us, always quietly waiting for us to respond. God, unlike the amateur potter, knows that creation cannot be forced onto center by brute pressure. The shaping of a life is a more delicate skill. God forever places a firm, strong hand against our wobbling lives. We are never forced onto our center; neither are we allowed to shift too far away from it. Is this not what we mean by prevenient grace? The Holy Spirit goes before us at every moment of our lives. The Spirit never imposes itself upon us, but it never lets us stray beyond a point where we can still respond to God.

The psalmist, not surprisingly, links this sense of God's ever-present guidance and support with a potter's image.

> Where can I escape from thy spirit?
>   Where can I flee from thy presence?
> If I climb up to heaven, thou art there;
>   if I make my bed in Sheol, again I find thee.
> If I take my flight to the frontiers
>   of the morning
>   or dwell at the limit of the western sea,
> even there thy hand will meet me
>   and thy right hand will hold me fast.
> . . . .
> Thou it was who didst fashion my inward parts;
> thou didst knit me together in my mother's
>   womb. . . .

> my body is no mystery to thee,
>   how I was secretly kneaded into shape
>   and patterned in the depths of the earth.
> —Psalm 139:7-10, 13, 15, NEB

God's presence is steady and firm. It never lurches unpredictably. It exerts a constant, gentle pressure upon us. It urges and guides us toward our center, but it never forces us there.

Paul makes this point in a more theological way. In Galatians 3:23-29 he argues that God gave the law to Israel as a kind of restraint in order that Israel might not stray too far from God before the Messiah came.

> Now before faith came, we were confined under the law, kept under restraint until faith should be revealed. So that the law was our custodian until Christ came, that we might be justified by faith. But now that faith has come, we are no longer under a custodian; for in Christ Jesus you are all sons of God, through faith.
> —Galatians 3:23-26

Paul suggests that God always restrains us gently and silently until we are ready to move onto our center in Christ. Like the potter who presses against the spinning clay until it is ready to center itself, God's prevenient grace presses against us until we are ready to find new life in Christ.

"The center." We use that phrase so glibly now. We describe our need to be "centered." We take time to get centered. We speak of it as if it were an easy and quick process. We believe that it is something we can master without difficulty. Yet learning to center the clay is one of the most difficult skills for many beginning potters to master. It takes physical strength and psychological steadiness. It is neither easy nor quick. It takes commitment and practice.

51

Moreover, when the potter has centered the clay, it only means that she is ready to begin. Those who speak so easily of being centered often imply that being centered is itself the only goal. They leave one feeling that to be centered is an end in itself. In pottery, however, it is only the place at which one begins the real work of building a vessel. It is the place at which we must arrive before we can begin our journey. It is never an end in itself. If it were, no pot would ever be made. The goal of centering the clay is to work it into a vessel that has some practical or aesthetic purpose. The potter centers the clay so that she can make an object of beauty or utility.

Similarly, when our lives are centered, it only means that the real work is about to begin.

> The riches and beauty of the spiritual landscape are not disclosed to us in order that we may sit in the sun parlour, be grateful for the excellent hospitality, and contemplate the glorious view . . . Our place is not the auditorium but the stage.[1]

Perhaps that is why we flee from flinging ourselves onto our center. To confront the real work demanded of us is too painful. The risks of being centered are too great. So we prefer to remain slightly off center. From that position we can enjoy ourselves and feel the satisfaction of playing at the religious life.

It is time to move beyond the centering. I kick the flywheel again with the toe of my right foot. The wheelhead picks up speed. I insert my thumb into the axis of the revolving clay. I am opening up the clay. If I do not drive my thumb into the very center of the clay, then everything else I do later will be slightly off center. The instability of this off-center opening may wreck the pot before it is completed. Gradually, using both hands, I make the opening wider and wider. I can insert both my hands into it. Now I am ready to lift up the pot's walls. The outer shape of the clay is only an extension of its center. I press from the center outward to make the walls. The outside is the surface of the inside. It is important to finish the pot's interior into a perfect cylinder. If the exterior is slightly misshapen, it can be trimmed later with a knife. The interior cannot be trimmed. The clay responds differently to the potter's touch at its center than it does when she touches the exterior. I am making a large, flared bowl. I notice a slight thickness on one wall. So I use my fingers on the interior to thin the clay. The bowl remains intact. If I had tried to touch only the exterior in the same way, the pot would have collapsed.

Life grows from some center, just as the pot takes form from its inner axis. Our strength and resiliency stem from this hidden center, just as the pot's strength arises out of its center. This is a basic life principle. It applies to all growth and development. A vast and complex living organism emerges from the center of one seed. Our lives begin when two cells merge into each other. A new cell is born, and within its center is all the information necessary to create a living person.

All changes in our lives occur from some unknown, interior center. The poet Rilke speaks of this mystery:

> The new thing in us, the added thing, has entered into our hearts, has gone into its inmost chamber and is not even there any more,—is already in our blood. And we do not learn what it was. We could easily be made to believe that nothing has happened, and yet we have changed, as a house changes into which a guest has entered. We cannot say who has come, perhaps we shall never know, but many signs indicate that the future enters into us in this way in order to transform itself in us long before it happens.[2]

This is why the tree of life and the tree of knowledge are at the center of the garden. Humanity is meant to live from the center. Humankind's limit is in the middle, the center of its existence rather than on the edge. The limits which we experience on the edges of our lives are merely the limits of the human condition, of our technology, of our possibilities. The limit in the middle of our lives is the limit of our being, of our true existence. We confuse these two limits and believe that they are one and the same. They are, however, very different. "In the knowledge of the limit on the edge there is constantly given the possibility of an inner boundlessness." In the knowledge of the limit that is in the middle of all existence, our being from every possible standpoint is limited. The Lord "is at once the limit and the middle of our existence."[3] This means that God, who gives life, is in the middle. In the middle of the world that God created for Adam and Eve was the tree, the Divine Presence. Adam and Eve had dominion over a world of which they were not the center but from whose center they derived their life. Our lives are meant to be a constant circling around this divine center of which we were never meant to take possession. This is the visual metaphor that dominates the early chapters of Genesis.

Pottery sheds light úpon this metaphor. The interior center reveals itself only in the midst of motion. The pot's center does not grow outward unless it is turning upon the wheelhead or rotating in the hands. It takes shape only in the movement of the clay around some center. The nearer a wheel-thrown pot comes to completion, the slower this motion is. The wheel's speed is greatest at the beginning. Just as the pot's inner arrangement takes form in the midst of motion, so the inner structure of our lives is discovered in the midst of action. The wheel's centrifugal force throws the clay outward toward the world, revealing the hidden core at its center. Without movement outward, the center remains hidden and powerless.

So too we must develop ourselves and take possession of our world in order to find our center. We will never find this inner center if we simply rest quietly and look inward. Yet we can also throw ourselves so unreservedly into our world that we lose all sense both of our inner center and of our true identity. There is a paradox here. Only when we lean out into the world does our inner center reveal itself. Only if we are firmly placed on this inner axis, however, will we be able to reach outward creatively. Teilhard de Chardin speaks of this same paradox when he balances the "divinizing of our activities" with the "divinizing of our passivities."

> I can only unite myself to the will of God (as endured passively) when all my strength is spent, at the point where my activity, fully extended and straining towards betterment (understood in ordinary human terms), finds itself continually counter-weighted by forces tending to halt me or overwhelm me. Unless I do everything I can to advance or resist, I shall not find myself at the required point—I shall not submit to God as much as I might have done or as much as he wishes. If, on the contrary, I persevere courageously, I shall rejoin God across evil, deeper down than evil; I shall draw close to him; and at that moment the optimum of my 'communion in resignation' necessarily coincides (by definition) with the maximum of fidelity to the human task.[4]

As we act upon the world outside of ourselves, we discover the center within us. Yet only if we move outward from some firm and deeply rooted center will our actions have a well-defined texture.

We must be infinitely attentive both to what is happening within us and to what we are doing in the world beyond us. This is why obedience becomes such a crucial concept in Christian formation. It is also why the prophets so frequently describe obedience in terms of a potter and the clay. Our English word *obedience* comes from the Latin root *audire*, "to listen." This root appears in words such as audience or audio. It means to be attentive, alert, and ready. The opposite of obedience, then, is not just disobedience. It is *absurdity*, to be deaf. We are either obedient or our lives are absurd. It is "being all ears" rather than "turning a deaf ear."

Obedience is not a passive stance. Neither is it blind, unreasoning, or uncritical. To probe and to explore is a sign of attentiveness and therefore of obedience. We grossly misstate the case when we make obedience a "blind surrender" of our wills. Because it involves attention, obedience is active and sometimes even exhausting. The Hebrew phrase that we regularly translate as "to obey" is *shama' le*. It means literally "to listen to." This is also true of the Greek. The usual word for obedience comes from the verbal root "to hear."

This double meaning clarifies many statements in the Bible. "He who has ears to hear, let him hear" (Matt. 11:15) quite literally means that those who truly hear what is being said must obey. "My sheep hear my voice, and I know them, and they follow me," says John 10:27. To disobey God's word in both the Hebrew Bible and the New Testament does not mean to have understood what God has said and then to turn away deliberately. It means that those who disobey simply did not hear in the first place. They were not attentive.

Simone Weil, the French philosopher and mystic

who died in 1943, describes this attentiveness as the key to the Christian concept of education. It is also the key to Christian prayer. Weil draws an analogy between prayer and learning mathematics or a foreign language:

> School children and students who love God should never say: "For my part I like mathematics"; "I like French"; "I like Greek." They should learn to like all these subjects, because all of them develop that faculty of attention which, directed toward God, is the very substance of prayer.[5]

Even if we hate geometry, Weil says, we can develop our aptitude for attention by wrestling with a theorem. "The habit of attention . . . is the substance of prayer." Weil goes on to suggest that to relate fully to our neighbors and to our world is also a habit of attention through which we learn to pray.

> The love of our neighbor in all its fullness simply means being able to say to him: "What are you going through?" . . . This way of looking is first of all attentive. The soul empties itself of all its own contents in order to receive into itself the being it is looking at, just as he is, in all his truth. Only he who is capable of attention can do this.[6]

Weil regards true attention as a form of obedience. To be attentive is to listen. It is to suspend our own thoughts. We leave ourselves detached and empty so that we may be open to the other. If we are truly listening to someone else, then we have stopped the mental chatter that circles endlessly around within our minds. We often hear someone speaking to us, but we are so busy listening to our own thoughts that we do

57

not truly listen to the speaker. There is room for others to enter into us only after we have become empty. This truth is the same whether we speak of the human heart or of the spinning clay.

The potter forms the vessel upon a wheel. The faster she kicks the flywheel, the more the centrifugal force drives the clay outward and the larger the void at the center becomes. If the clay clung rigidly to its own center, it would never become a pot. The clay massed at the center must flow outward and upward to form the walls. Unless it is willing to become empty at its core, the pot can never see its walls curve gracefully upward. When we insist upon remaining at the center of our lives, we leave room neither for God, who is our true center, nor for other people and issues. To cling to our ego-centers is not merely to refuse to reach out beyond ourselves. It is also to leave no room for God within us.

Sometime near the end of the fifth century an anonymous Christian wrote a tract called "On The Divine Names." This unknown author has become known as Pseudo-Dionysius the Areopagite, since he claimed to be the Dionysius whom Paul converted at the Athenean Areopagus. Pseudo-Dionysius gives the following illustration for how we, God, and the world interrelate.

> All the radii of a circle are concentrated into a single unity in the centre, and this point contains all the straight lines brought together within itself and unified to one another, and to the one starting-point from which they began. Even so are they a perfect unity in the centre itself, and . . . departing further are differenced further, and, in fact, the nearer they are to the centre, so much the more are they united to it and to one another, and the more they are separated from it the more they are separated from one another.[7]

Pseudo-Dionysius' point is really quite simple. The closer we draw to others, the closer we draw to God. The farther away we move from God, the farther we move from others. We are no different than the clay. When we are willing to abandon ourselves and to fling ourselves outward in compassion and in service, we find that we have made room not just for others in our lives but also for God in our hearts. The energy that we had massed in our own little center is spent on others, leaving an open space where God may enter. From this same God-infused center also flows the renewing energy that allows us to keep loving and serving in the world. This is why John Wesley affirmed that true faith issues in good works. It is also why Baron von Hugel ordered his spiritual directee, Evelyn Underhill, to serve several days a week in a skid row soup kitchen when she was having trouble with her spiritual life.

True obedience, then, is both a listening to what we hear within us and to what we hear beyond us. It is being attentive to those we encounter in our daily lives. It is creating the empty, open space within us where we can hear God speak.

> You know well enough that if you put yourselves at the disposal of a master, to obey him, you are slaves of the master whom you obey; and this is true whether you serve sin, with death as its result; or obedience, with righteousness as its result. But God be thanked, you, who once were slaves of sin, have yielded whole-hearted obedience to the pattern of teaching to which you were made subject, and, emancipated from sin, have become slaves of righteousness . . . making for a holy life.
>
> —Romans 6:16-19, NEB

Paul makes obedience not only a careful hearing of what God has to say but also an attentive presence in the midst of the world, making for a holy life.

If reality is constructed in this way, where is God to be encountered? The general tendency has been to establish a rigid either/or line as to where God is found. We have pursued a ruthless division of the world into matter and mind, body and spirit, public and private. Our scriptures, however, suggest a both/and approach. The Hebrew Bible preserves the memories of two very different mountaintop revelations. The first is external, objective, and public. Moses went up to the top of Mount Sinai. The people heard the Voice and saw the pillar of fire and smoke. This experience at Sinai has set the tone for much of Western, revealed religion. It emphasizes that which is beyond us. A very different recollection is transmitted to us through the story of Elijah's long journey to the mountain of God. According to this story, God is not present in the external, visible demonstrations but rather in the "still small voice." The Hebrew phrase used to describe this voice suggests the barely audible, internal sound of our breathing. This revelation, then, is personal and internal. In contrast to the Moses tradition in which God speaks from without, the Elijah tradition implies that God speaks subjectively from within.

The ideal, of course, would be to have an encounter where the inner and the outer, the objective and the subjective, are held in equilibrium. The source of God's encounter with us would be everywhere. It is inside of us and outside of us because the two dimensions are really one and the same. The one who speaks from the top of the mountain is also heard within each person's heart.

This is precisely the conviction of the New Testament when it confesses that Jesus is the Christ. Israel was torn between the outer and the inner modes of divine presence. One mode of presence stressed the objective vision of God. This mode found its most zealous advocates among the priestly classes who served in the Temple or among royal circles who saw the king as a visible, objective sign of God's presence. The second mode of presence emphasized the inner voice. God's voice is heard, but nothing is seen. The prophetic tradition, represented by figures such as Elijah or Amos, nurtured this insight.

In Jesus Christ there is one who is both priest and prophet. Jesus is the Word that dwells among us in the flesh and whose glory is seen. Voice and Vision are united. Public and private, body and spirit, inner and outer, are all unified. The illusion of division and separation is abolished. Because this separation between God's modes of presence is overcome, all barriers are dissolved.

Paul expresses this conviction in a variety of ways. If anyone is in Christ, they are a new creation where the old worldly standards have ceased to count in our estimate of others (2 Cor. 5:11-17). Christ has broken down the dividing wall of hostility, destroying our securities built upon rigid definitions of inside and outside (Eph. 2:11-22).

> Whoever partakes of the flesh of Christ has all sorts of barriers dissolved in him together with sin and death. He is thus made one with every man, a new man, newly and purely created in a manner analogous to the image of Christ . . . . In other words, the Church, by nature of its catholicity, is against all sorts of discriminations, division, isolation, and even all that causes division, whatever its source may be, whether within man or outside of him.[8]

There is, however, a very significant difference between the clay and our lives. The pot, as it empties from its center, has no real choice. It is simply obeying the laws of centrifugal force. True freedom and true obedience are, therefore, identical. Obedience is not a lessening of our freedom. It is a heightened form of it, a rising to our destiny. Freedom is not license but rather the capacity to choose to obey the urgings of our deepest center. Freedom, Spinoza somewhere writes, is the recognition of necessity. At our best moments we live by a freedom that issues from our obedience. This trusting obedience is "not an abdication of freedom but a mature use of freedom."9 We do not understand this and often resist obedience to God in the name of a perverted freedom. Properly understood, we have no more freedom than the tree that grows in our yard. We are free only to be who we really are or to pretend that we are someone or something else. We are never free actually to be someone or something else. True freedom is ultimately doing in obedience that which we are intended to do and to be. The clay flows outward naturally. We stubbornly cling to our shored-up center in the name of a false freedom.

We have too often severed our freedom from our obedience. This corrupted freedom means nothing more than doing what we want to do when we want to do it. John Milton rightly understood the true nature of freedom as obedience. Freedom is not set apart from obedience. After Adam and Eve eat the forbidden fruit and the sentence of expulsion is delivered, an angel comes to them and conveys some last minute instructions. Adam replies:

> Henceforth I learn, that to obey is best,
> And love with fear the only God, to walk
> As in his presence, ever to observe
> His providence, and on him sole depend,
> Merciful over all his works, with good
> Still overcoming evil, and by small

> Accomplishing great things, by things deemed
>   weak
> Subverting worldly strong, and worldly wise
> By simply meek

The angel then commends Adam:

> This having learned, thou has attained the sum
> Of wisdom; hope no higher, though all the stars
> Thou knew'st by name . . . . only add
> Deeds to thy knowledge answerable, add faith,
> Add virtue, patience, temperance, add love,
> By name to come called Charity, the soul
> Of all the rest; then wilt thou not be loath
> To leave this Paradise, but shalt possess
> A paradise within thee, happier far.[10]

Obedience is the path of highest freedom because it leads to all the fruit of the Spirit. It leads to our becoming who we were truly created to be. To obey is to possess a paradise within.

The conflict between freedom and obedience is falsely stated. There is a point of passivity or of receptivity at the very heart of all willing. There is a kind of interior necessity that is deeper and more personal than any independent choice. Ivan in Dostoevski's *The Brothers Karamazov* says, "If God does not exist, everything is permissible." He is really saying that if there is only our ego-center and nothing more, then there is no ultimate validity for either our freedom or our willing. Reinhold Niebuhr wrote, "Man is most free in the discovery that he is not free."[11] Even Paul links freedom with obedience.

> You, my friends, were called to be free men; only do not turn your freedom into licence for your lower nature, but be servants to one another in love. For the

whole law can be summed up in a single command-
ment: "Love your neighbour as yourself."
—Galatians 5:13-14, NEB

The highest freedom is not license but obedience. It is
an attentive concern for others that arises out of a
deeply inward centering. Even as the clay is free only
to obey the potter's hands, humankind was created to
live in obedience to the Divine Potter's touch. To live is
to obey.

Yet through humankind's tragic twisting of its
freedom, we may now willingly choose not to obey.
We may will ourselves to live at our own partial and
fragmented center rather than from the divine center
but when we do this, we choose for ourselves death
rather than life. Conversely, obedient attentiveness
immerses us in all the vitality, movement, and
creativity of our world. Its alternative is absurdity.
When we live at our own center, we limit all our
experiencing to ourselves alone. We cut ourselves off
from the stimulation and growth that contact with the
fullness of life brings. Those who are deaf to the world
are truly absurd. They are the living dead. The
traditional folk wisdom of Israel, preserved in the
Book of Proverbs, clearly understood this choice.

> Now, my sons, listen to me,
> listen to instruction and grow wise,
>   do not reject it.
> Happy is the man who keeps to my ways,
> happy the man who listens to me,
> watching daily at my threshold
> with his eyes on the doorway;
> for he who finds me finds life
> and wins favour with the Lord,
> while he who finds me not, hurts himself,
> and all who hate me are in love with death.
> —Proverbs 8:32-36, NEB

Throwing The Pot

I begin to pull up the clay. I press it between my left index finger, which rests on the pot's inner wall, and the first knuckle of my right hand, which is on the pot's outside. As I lift my hands, the clay wall rises upward. My left thumb is braced against my right wrist so that my hands remain the same distance apart. This position assures that the wall will have a consistent thickness. I repeat the process three or four times. Each time I bring more clay up from the base and the center. Each time the walls grow taller. The clay responds eagerly to my touch, yet it still has a mind of its own. I must use water to lubricate the clay as I work with it. If I use too much water, the walls weaken and slump. If I work too long on the same piece, it becomes tired and collapses. If I misjudge the amount of clay I am working with, I make the walls so thin that they wilt and fall inward.

I have formed an image within my mind of the pot that I want to make. Sometimes the clay refuses to cooperate with my intentions. The complex intercommunication between the clay, my hands, and my mind breaks down. I envision the walls turning gracefully outward and then back inward to form a narrow collar. I spread the walls outward, but they refuse to collar back at the top. The envisioned vase wobbles off center and collapses. The graceful object that I saw with my inner eye is no more than a blob of wet clay. I must tear it off the wheel and begin anew with a different ball of clay.

It is as if the clay seeks to create a bowl even though I want a vase. Unable to agree between ourselves, the result is spoiled and wasted. Is this what our Creator feels when we refuse to grow according to our divine image, careen wildly along our own path, and finally topple upon ourselves? This tangled encounter between potter and clay has provided one of the most fertile images in prophetic literature.

Judah was limping toward its final destruction. King Josiah, who had tried to vitalize the nation by a return to the ancient Deuteronomic laws, had been killed in 609 BCE. Leading his troops into battle against Pharaoh Neco and the Egyptian armies, Josiah had lost his life. His son Jehoahaz ruled three months before he was replaced by another of Josiah's sons whom the Egyptians found more acceptable: Jehoiakim (2 Kings 23:31-37). Jehoiakim, in addition to being a despot and paganizer, did little to stop Judah's drift toward extinction. The prophet Jeremiah could see no hope for the nation. God had tried again and again to call the people back from the brink of destruction. They refused to listen. God was weary of relenting and would soon allow events to take their natural course.

This prophetic truth is poignantly described in Jeremiah 18. Seeing a potter seated at his wheel, Jeremiah perceives that the people are clay in the Divine Potter's hands. If the clay vessel is spoiled because of its resistance and imperfections, then the potter will cast it aside and make another vessel. If the people refuse to be molded by God and insist on pursuing their own plans, then they will perish.

These are the words which came to Jeremiah from the Lord: Go down at once to the potter's house, and there I will tell you what I have to say. So I went down to the potter's house and found him working at the wheel. Now and then a vessel he was making out of the clay would be spoilt in his hands, and then he would start again and mould it into another vessel to his liking. Then the word of the Lord came to me: Can I not deal with you, Israel, says the Lord, as the potter deals with his clay? You are clay in my hands like the clay in his, O house of Israel.

—Jeremiah 18:1-6, NEB

Life is not a matter of change and random events. History is not like the rocks on the seashore that are shaped by wind and water. It bears the imprint of God's own shaping and forming hands.

Jeremiah's warning, however, went unheeded. Judah's weak and vacillating King Zedekiah joined in a futile rebellion against Babylon. In 588 BCE King Nebuchadrezzar laid siege to Jerusalem. The city resisted heroically until it fell during the summer of 587/86. Babylonian troops captured Zedekiah as he fled the city. They brought him to Nebuchadrezzar's headquarters in Riblah. Having witnessed the execution of his sons, Zedekiah was blinded and taken in chains to Babylon. Massive deportations to Babylon followed these events. Others fled to Egypt. Judah disappeared as an independent nation (2 Kings 25). Jeremiah's terrible prophecy was fulfilled.

Unexpected events soon began to reverse Israel's fortunes. By 550 BCE King Cyrus of Media had consolidated his power. Cyrus marched against Lydia in 547/46 BCE and conquered most of Asia Minor. Persia's ambitions now turned toward the dying Babylonian empire. An unknown Israelite prophet whose writings have been appended to the scroll of

Isaiah believed that Cyrus was the messiah who would deliver Israel from captivity. When the exiles scoffed at him, he reminded them that God shapes human destiny as the potter shapes the clay. What God has purposed cannot be frustrated. Second Isaiah, prophet to the exiles in Babylon, returns to Jeremiah's ceramic metaphor.

> Will the pot contend with the potter,
> or the earthenware with the hand that shapes it?
> Will the clay ask the potter what he is making?
> or his handiwork say to him, "You have no skill"?
> Will the babe say to his father,
> "What are you begetting?",
> or to his mother, "What are you bringing to birth?"
> Thus says the Lord, Israel's Holy One, his maker:
> Would you dare question me concerning my
> children,
> or instruct me in my handiwork?
> I alone, I made the earth
> and created man upon it.
> —Isaiah 45:9-12, NEB

Second Isaiah links creation with redemption. The one who created the world will return to redeem it. His potter echoes not only Jeremiah's vision but also the potter of Genesis 2:19.

Jeremiah, Genesis, and Second Isaiah all complain that the clay often attempts to disobey the Divine Potter's vision. Adam and Eve were molded by the cosmic potter but rejected their maker's creative intentions, wobbled uncertainly, and fell in upon themselves. The Genesis accounts make it clear that the Fall arises out of humankind's attempt to go beyond God's ultimate designs, replacing the divine constructs with its own. Unwilling to live from the center, they seek to live at the center. The agent of this rebellion is the serpent. Curiously, the text nowhere states that the serpent is Satan. In fact, it explicitly calls the serpent "a creature of God." The serpent also introduces itself in the name of God. The serpent bears with it the word of God and claims to expound and to interpret this divine word: Have you really understood what God means when God says, "Do not eat"? Isn't it possible that what God really means is . . . ? The serpent thus implies that the revealed commandment of God is incomplete. The highest freedom is not obedience to the commandment of God but the freedom to interpret what God means.

> The decisive point is that this question suggests to man that he should go behind the Word of God and establish what it is by himself, out of his understanding of the being of God. For the sake of the true God it seems to want to sweep aside the given Word of God . . . Beyond this given Word of God the serpent pretends somehow to know something about the profundity of the true God who is so badly misrepresented in this human word . . . The serpent's question was a thoroughly religious one. But with the first religious question in the world evil has come upon the scene . . . Man is expected to be judge of God's word instead of simply hearing and doing it.[1]

The serpent suggests that it is possible to know something about God beyond God's given word. Adam and Eve renounce the word of God that constantly flows to them out of the middle and limit of their lives. They decide instead to occupy this middle and to judge for themselves about life's meaning and possibilities. "Therefore man's being like God is disobedience in the form of obedience, it is will to

69

power in the form of service, it is desire to be creator in the form of creatureliness, it is being dead in the form of life."[2]

Adam and Even have left the path of true obedience. They are no longer attentive to the word that speaks from the center. They no longer respond with attentive ears to the inner word that seeks to shape them. They cannot listen to this divine word because the endless mental chatter of their own questioning overshadows it. They are asking questions, demanding interpretations, posing problems. Their own confused flood of mental possibilities and constructs sweeps away the divine possibilities that throb quietly within them.

They believe that they can discover a new and better way to shape their lives. They confuse the divine center and its possibilities with their own willful options. The serpent, after all, promises them that they will be "like God." So being like God is set over against being the image of God. Humankind as the image of God lives from the center but not at the center. Humanity as being like God tries to live from the depths of its own imperfect knowledge. The desperate feature of Adam and Eve's situation is that even as they live out of themselves, they are imprisoned within themselves. They can desire only themselves. They crave only themselves. Adam and Eve must now be the creators of their own lives. This is why John Milton has lust and sexual passion as the first consequences of the Fall.

> But come, so well refresh'd, now let us play,
> As meet is, after such delicious fare;
> For never did thy beauty, since the day
> I saw thee first and wedded thee, adorned
> With all perfections, so inflame my sense
> With ardor to enjoy thee, fairer now

Than ever, bounty of this virtuous tree.
  So said he, and forbore not glance or toy
Of amorous intent, well understood
Of Eve, whose eye darted contagious fire.
. . . .
There they their fill of love and love's disport
Took largely, of their mutual guilt the seal,
The solace of their sin.[3]

The serpent's promise is true. Adam and Eve become "like God." Even as God is a creator of life, they now must create their own life. They are responsible for their own life project. They must live out of their own fragmented selves.

Humankind is now the lord of its world, but it is the mute, silenced, dead world of its own ego. Now that they have made themselves gods, they no longer have a God who infuses new, creative possibilities into the world. The more serious and frantic their attempt to recover the lost image of God, the greater their contradiction of God. "Their misshapen form, modelled after the god they have invented for themselves, grows more and more like the image of Satan, though they are unaware of it."[4] This is the tragic consequence of the Fall. We are responsible for a life project that we do not have the resources either to initiate or to complete. Thus we are doomed to live without the possibility of living.

Having excluded God from our inner center, we also have excluded the creative and alternative possibilities that God constantly infuses into our lives. Dominated by a life that is only being like God, we must create our own paltry and pallid substitutes. We become self-generating, but we have nothing genuine to create. We attempt to be the creator and sustainer of our own lives. This passion to be our own creators prevents us from yielding our lives to that original center that was both middle and limit to our lives.

To yield is to disperse one's shored-up center, to let down one's guard, one's character armor, and to admit one's lack of self-sufficiency. Our passion to be our own creator is a dynamic fantasy that blankets in forgetfulness our lack of a genuine center that would assure us a victory over life. To yield

> represents nothing less than the abandonment of the *causa-sui* project, the deepest, completest, total emotional admission that there is no strength within oneself, no power to bear the superfluity of experience. To yield is to admit that support has to come from outside oneself and that justification for one's life has to come totally from some self-transcending web in which one consents to be suspended—as a child in its hammock-cradle, glaze-eyed in helpless, dependent admiration of the cooing mother.[5]

Our passion to be our own creators is the root of our sinfulness. We refuse to yield our shored-up center to that greater Center from which our life truly comes. This is why death is the fruit of sin.

Sin is the total life project of trying to be one's own center, one's own creator. It is what Paul calls justification by works. The pious Pharisee sought to create an identity through obedience to the law. The inquiring Greek sought it by constructing a philosophy in which the self can be located and understood. "Jews call for miracles, Greeks look for wisdom; but we proclaim Christ—yes, Christ nailed to the cross . . . he is the power of God and the wisdom of God" (1 Cor. 1:22-24, NEB). We still seek the same paths that the inquiring Greek and the pious Pharisee forged before us. We try to wind experiences and knowledge around ourselves and to cover ourselves with accomplishments in order to make ourselves visible both in our own eyes and before the world. We convince ourselves that we are the sum total of our accomplishments. Paul goes on to affirm that this path leads only to sin and to death. Jesus Christ, Paul writes, frees us from this illusion of self-generation. To place our faith in Jesus Christ is to yield our false and feeble centers and to admit that our true Center lies beyond us in that self-transcending web in which we are all suspended. Paul reminds his readers that he knows how to play the game of being one's own center and of trying to generate one's own life.

> If anyone thinks to base his claims on externals, I could make a stronger case for myself: circumcised on my eighth day, Israelite by race, of the tribe of Benjamin, a Hebrew born and bred; in my attitude to the law, a Pharisee; in pious zeal, a persecutor of the church; in legal rectitude, faultless.
>
> —Philippians 3:4-6, NEB

He then goes on to assert that this passion for our life project means nothing. Our lives find their deepest purpose only in Christ Jesus, who restores our original centeredness in God.

> But all such assets I have written off because of Christ. I would say more: I count everything sheer loss, because all is far outweighed by the gain of knowing Christ Jesus my Lord, for whose sake I did in fact lose everything. I count it so much garbage, for the sake of gaining Christ and finding myself incorporate in him, with no righteousness of my own, no legal rectitude, but the righteousness which comes from faith in Christ, given by God in response to faith.
>
> —Philippians 3:7-11, NEB

Paul echoes closely the language of Jeremiah and Second Isaiah in Romans as he struggles to express this relationship between justification by works and justification by faith.

> Who are you, sir, to answer God back? Can the pot speak to the potter and say, "Why did you make me like this?"? Surely the potter can do what he likes with the clay. Is he not free to make out of the same lump two vessels, one to be treasured, the other for common use?
>
> —Romans 9:20-21, NEB

We anxiously build up a life facade. We create structures and signs of our worth and value. We are like the pot that tries to build itself into a treasured, beautiful vessel rather than let God shape it according to divine purposes. Sin characterizes our lives because we are not content to let the Divine Potter shape our lives. Instead we try to decide what shall be made from our lump of clay.

There is another hidden danger here that is not immediately apparent. Seeping through the cracks in our facade is the awareness of how fragile our lives are. We vaguely sense the instability and shoddiness of our life project. We comprehend that we cannot complete the project we have undertaken. There is only one escape from this dilemma. We look around us for someone stronger, more powerful than we are. We then endow this person with authority over us. The emptier we feel, the more we people our world with omnipotent, magical helpers. We grasp the fact that we stand in need of something beyond us, but we look for the nearest support. Instead of lifting our eyes to an ultimate horizon, we latch onto a person, a cause, a movement.

People need a "beyond." Yet they do not know where to look for it. They reach for the nearest one and this fulfills their need, but it also limits and enslaves them. The object that appears to fulfill us ends up stunting our development. "You can ask the question: What kind of beyond does this person try to expand in; and how much individuation does he achieve in it?"[6]

Even when we begin to recognize that we cannot live out of our own center, we seldom yield to the divine Center. We seek some interim solution. We find another fragmented center beyond our own and submit to it. We abandon the attempt to live from our own center and settle for living out of someone else's. We want to be justified, to know that our self-creation is not in vain. So we look to someone or something that will pronounce absolution. The result of this identity confusion is submission to authority.

This attempt to live out of someone else's center is our common experience of obedience. This obedience is oppressive and distorted. It makes it nearly impossible for us to enter into that basic, God-given unity of true obedience which is the freedom to obey an inner necessity. We become so suspicious of all obedience that we cannot distinguish appropriate obedience from that which is not appropriate. This false obedience has elements of genuine obedience because it does involve an attentive listening to the other. It is false because it has as its center something other than God. Our common definition of obedience, therefore, becomes submission to an external authority. Our models of obedience are purely authoritarian models because we depict obedience as this self-other relationship. The person who issues the orders is portrayed in images such as father, mother, ruler, owner, commander. The one who obeys is a child, subject, slave, soldier. This authoritarian unfreedom is the opposite of biblical obedience.

When we submit to this sort of false obedience, we have entered into a truly demonic world. Sadly, this truncated obedience is a basic element in the structure of our social life. In order to study the act of obeying, Stanley Milgram set up an experiment at Yale University. The conception was simple. Two people come to a psychology laboratory to take part in a study of memory and learning. One of them is designated as a teacher. The other is the learner. The experimenter explains that the study tests the effects of punishment on learning. The learner is conducted into a room, seated in a chair, and strapped to electrodes. The teacher is shown all of this and even receives a mild shock from the electrode so that he understands how the experiment works. The learner is to complete a series of word pairs. Whenever she makes an error, she will receive a shock. The teacher administers these shocks from the next room. The teacher sits before a panel with thirty switches that increase the voltage from 15 volts to 450 volts. With every mistake, the voltage is increased to the next level.

The experiment, however, is not what it appears to be. The learner is really an actor. The experiment seeks to test not the effects of punishment on learning but the limits of obedience. How far will the teacher proceed in a situation in which he or she is ordered to inflict pain on a protesting victim. At 75 volts the learner grunts. At 120 volts there are verbal complaints about pain. At 150 volts the learner demands to be released from the experiment. At 250 volts his response is nothing more than an agonized scream. The teacher gradually experiences conflict. The learner's pain compels him to quit. On the other hand, the experimenter, representing legitimate authority, orders him to continue. What are the limits of obedience to authority? Those who proposed the experiment predicted that all subjects would defy authority when the voltage reached dangerous or painful levels. The results surprised them. Of the 40 initial subjects, 26 continued punishing the learner until they reached 450 volts. At 300 volts the laboratory walls resounded as the victim pounded his fists in protest. After 315 volts the learner no longer even answered questions. Still, over one half of all subjects continued to administer the shock.

Milgram's conclusions shed much light on the roots of our false and demonic obedience. He applies a cybernetic, systems approach to the problem and concludes:

> The critical shift in functioning is reflected in an alteration of attitude. Specifically, the person entering an authority system no longer views himself as acting out of his own purposes but rather comes to see himself as an agent for executing the wishes of another person. . . . In this condition the individual no longer views himself as responsible for his own actions but defines himself as an instrument for carrying out the wishes of another.[7]

This is the false obedience that arises from our attempt to live from another person's center or a group's center. It is a far cry from what the Hebrew Bible and the New Testament mean by faithful obedience.

In the Hebrew Bible obedience is always related to justice. Under no circumstances is it related to the ruler in a completely authoritarian manner. It always has a particular objective content. "God has told you what is good; and what is it that the Lord asks of you? Only to act justly, to love loyalty, to walk wisely before your God" (Micah 6:8, NEB). The object of obedience is a world and a humanity that are shaped directly by God for the purposes of restoring creation to its original wholeness. A purely authoritarian form of obedience is misleading because it loses sight of these purposes. Obedience becomes an end in itself. The Hebrew Bible never makes of obedience this kind of goal and end unto itself.

Paul makes a linguistic distinction between obedience as a religious decision and obedience in the sense of submission to authorities in the social and political spheres. The obedience that can be equated with faith, as we have noted, has its linguistic root in hearing (Rom. 16:26). The second word refers to submission to authority and is related to an "ordering" or "status" root form (Rom. 13:1). This second word has its source in military circles and refers to the positioning of troops in rank during battle. We must never confuse the obedience of faith with this submission to authority.

Authentic existence, according to Paul, comes neither from resting in our own center nor from trying to rest in the center of another person or cause. These modes of life are truly *ab-surd*. They are sin and death. Paul elsewhere provides other definitions of obedience and disobedience that reflect this conviction. Disobedience is the refusal to accept our justification by grace through faith. It is continuing to live as if the gift of life were something we achieve by ourselves. Faith is practically synonymous with obedience where obedience means a willingness to live attentively before a gracious God who bestows life freely. When Paul understands faith as obedience, he does not regard the gospel as a command. It is a message which makes a claim on the hearer. "To trust is to commit oneself . . . To trust a message is to rely on it, to act on it, to be shaped by it . . . Our identity is constituted by the pattern or network of trust, the configuration of that to which we are committed because we deem it trustworthy."[8]

Paul elsewhere connects hearing with heeding. When he mentions how the Thessalonians came to have faith, he speaks of their obedience (1 Thess. 1:8). In Romans 1:8 he writes of "your faith" and in Romans 16:19 he speaks of "your obedience." He clearly means the same thing in both instances. In Romans 1:5 he mentions the "obedience of faith."

When we are obedient to the deep configuration of being that we name God, then we are exercising the gift of faith. This faith leads to authentic existence. It is a dynamic trust in God, our living center. This trust is not the same thing as reliability. Reliability rests upon merely rational and functional proofs. Trust arises from a more personal encounter that requires that it not be tested, judged, or proven. When trust is tested for its reliability, it dissolves. We in our culture confuse reliability with trust. We speak about trust when what we mean is reliability. This sort of trust becomes the truth of control and prediction rather than the truth of love and belonging. This confusion makes it very difficult for us to understand the biblical meanings of trust, faith, and obedience.

We destroy the certainty of trustworthiness by wanting to verify and to quantify it. On rational grounds we can be sure of someone's reliability. This is a functional category. It means that in certain social, economic, or political relationships this person will probably behave in a predictable way, a way on which I can rely. This functional reliability is based upon how I know this person has behaved in the past. Reliability is predicated upon past performance alone. Trust, on the other hand, is future-oriented. It relates to my faith in this person's consistency no matter what the future may hold. Trust is not verifiable, and the desire for verification will destroy it. We are not shaped by what we rely upon. We are shaped by what or whom we trust. Obedience that rests upon a confusion of reliability with trust will ultimately decay into an authoritarian unfreedom, which is never to be confused with true obedience.

Faith, trust, and obedience all converge around a core experience that eludes precise definition. This experience of authentic existence, however, is at the heart of the Christian vision. Jesus is above all else the faithful servant who is obedient unto death. In him the possibility of life in the image of God rather than merely life as being like God reappears in human history. Christian existence is about our transformation into this image of God made real for us in Jesus Christ. Christ opens up for us this possibility of genuine obedience. Christ restores the potential reintegration of our fragmented lives upon the horizon of human experience.

C   H   A   P   T   E   R   5

Firing
The Bisque Ware

The clay pots have been wrapped loosely in plastic and left to dry on open shelves. Gradually the air dries them until they are leather hard. Any last-minute changes will now be made by trimming the clay. The potter uses a sharp knife to trim excess clay from the pot as it rotates slowly on the wheelhead. Another trimming tool may be used to shape a footring that will give a bowl some added stability. It is easier to trim the footring when the pot is leather hard than when the wet clay is still on the wheel. Sometimes trying to throw a footring on the wheel takes longer than throwing the rest of the vessel. The potter may also trim her pot in order to correct some visual flaw in its exterior. Once the trimming is completed, the pot is ready at last for firing in the kiln. This is the first of two firings that the clay must undergo. The first, bisque firing, occurs before the pot is glazed. The second and final firing is a glaze firing that fuses the glaze into the clay.

Bisque firing changes the clay's chemical composition. It increases the pot's durability while leaving it porous enough to absorb the glaze. Some potters apply the glaze directly to the unfired, leather-hard pot. Most, however, prefer to bisque fire the pot first.

81

The extreme temperatures at which bisque firing takes place make the clay much stronger. The firing reduces the possibility that the still-plastic pot will be damaged during its decoration and glazing.

Bisque firing seeks two results. First, the chemically combined water that is suspended in the clay will be extruded. Second, a complex chemical reaction called the cristobalite conversion takes place. The mineral silica comes in different forms. Firing transforms the clay's silica from one state to another. It converts the quartz or free silica in its crystalline phase into free silica of the cristobalite phase. Cristobalite allows the clay to shrink. When the pot is glaze fired, this shrinkage factor is important. The raw glaze will also shrink during firing. Thus, the clay pot must contract at roughly the same percentage as the glaze. If it does not, then the glaze will craze and crack on the pot's surface. The cristobalite factor helps assure successful glazing.

Bisque firing must begin slowly in order to allow the water to escape from the clay as it changes into steam. If the firing begins too rapidly, the sudden pressure of the steam will blast large flakes of clay from the vessel's wall. The conversion of steam usually takes place at a temperature between 840° F and 1110° F when the kiln begins to turn dull red. Organic impurities in the clay decompose and fire away at about 390° F to 750° F. Other chemical impurities such as sulphur trioxide, which combines with moisture to form sulphuric acid, and fluorine begin to fire away at temperatures of 1650° F and above. The bisque firing temperatures must be controlled from rising too high, too quickly. The higher the firing temperature, the more the clay's porosity is reduced. The pot needs this porosity in order for the glaze to adhere.

Fire is the agent of this transformation. Only fire can

transform the raw clay into earthenware, stoneware, or porcelain. Our word *ceramic* derives from the Greek word *keramos*, "burnt up." Perhaps fire's capacity to transform whatever it touches accounts for humanity's fascination with it. Perhaps it has been fire's capacity to transform things quickly and permanently. Fire is the quick, the ag-ile, Ag-nis, ig-nis.[1]

> Fire is for the man who is contemplating it an example of a sudden change or development and an example of a circumstantial development. Less monotonous and less abstract than flowing water, even more quick to grow and to change than the young bird we watch every day in its nest in the bushes, fire suggests the desire to change, to speed up the passage of time, to bring all of life to its conclusion, to its hereafter . . . . it magnifies human destiny; it links the small to the great, the hearth to the volcano, the life of a log to the life of a world.[2]

The changes wrought by fire are not just changes in appearance. They are genuine transformations of substance. That which has been licked by fire has a different taste in our mouth. That which fire has touched retains a red, fiery glow within it. Through fire everything changes. When we want something to change, we call upon fire.

If all that changes slowly may be explained by life, all that changes quickly can be explained by fire. Fire is the ultra-living element. It includes everything within it. It is intimate and it is universal. It lives in our heart and in the sky. It rises from the depths of matter and offers itself to us with the warmth of love. "Among all phenomena, it is really the only one to which there can be so definitely attributed the opposing values of good and evil. It shines in Paradise. It burns in Hell. It is gentleness and torture. It is cookery and it is apocalypse."[3] Fire both fascinates us and frightens us. It inspires great hope and great comfort. It terrorizes us when it rages out of control.

My earliest memories revolve around these dual aspects of fire. When I was a very young child, my bed was in our living room during the winter months. The upstairs bedrooms had no heat. So in cold weather we drew closer to the glowing stoves that radiated warmth into our living room and kitchen. The living-room stove was a large coal burner. My father would build up the fire just before bedtime, mixing corncobs with the coal to add to the fire's intensity. The room would be blanketed in darkness, but all night long the tiny glass windows would emit a warm, comforting red glow. I could see the flames dancing happily behind them. Sometimes I would awaken from a nightmare, feeling lost and alone. I would look into the rhythmic incandescence of those glowing windows and feel warm and safe.

Only later did I discover how destructive fire could be. I stepped out onto our porch one summer night and saw the southeastern sky aglow with a great blaze. The fire shone against the night sky and extended out over the broad expanse of the cornfields. We drove along lonely country roads and, like modern-day Magi, followed the lights in the sky. Eventually we came to an intense, hungry fire that was consuming a rural grain elevator. The tall brick and wooden structure had collapsed, spilling tons of smoking, burning grain across the highway. The ragged remains of the brick tower shed an angry, red incandescence on the assembled firefighters. Volunteer fire departments from several towns had answered the call for help. Everyone, however, stood helplessly at a distance and watched the conflagration consume its own body. I had nightmares about fire for weeks afterwards.

Fire is the little, savage animal that is so easy to capture and to tame. It is a pet to play with and to fondle. Yet fire lives by consuming, and it consumes only in breathing life into its fiery heat. Fire makes the kettle sing on the stove. It turns the bread golden brown. We know the fire that sweetens life: the fire of burning leaves, of winter chimneys, of tobacco rising from a pipe. We know also the fire that rages and devours everything in its path: the fire that falls from the sky and kills, the fire that leaves our homes and forests a heap of ashes.

Without fire and light, life might never have begun. In 1953 a young University of Chicago biochemist named Stanley Miller set out to test one theory of how life on earth began. He took the molecules assumed to have been plentiful in our infant atmosphere: hydrogen, methane, ammonia, and water vapor. These were mixed together in a special chamber. Into this primeval sea he introduced regular electric charges, approximating as nearly as possible the effects of natural lightning. Soon the mixture had created the building blocks of all life: nucleic acids and amino acids. Fire from the sky had transformed the molecules so that they might produce life.[4] Fire is capable of effecting changes in substance and appearance. What nature matures slowly, fire changes at an unsuspected speed. How can we work faster than nature? How can we intervene in the cosmic processes? By fire. Fire does all this faster than nature. It also creates something entirely new that did not exist prior to its action.

Neither the fire that comforts and assures us nor the fire before which we flee in terror is the potter's fire. The potter's fire, like the potter's wheel, is a unique creation. The potter takes this destructive, dangerous force and converts it into a creative power. The more tightly the potter imprisons her fire within the kiln, the more she feeds and provokes it. The potter's fire has its closest analogy in the farmer's fire. The farmer sets ablaze his harvested fields in order both to purify them and to fertilize them. He burns away the weeds and leaves a thin layer of ash upon the soil. This is likewise the twin purpose of the potter's fire.

This is also the fire of human transformation. Christian transformation is our passage through the fire of divine love. It is the yielding, in obedience and trust, of our own partial center. It is the transition from inner fire to celestial light. Fire smolders in our souls more surely than it does under the ashes. This is the fire of our passion, of our love. A popular song calls for the beloved to "light my fire." A romantic evening is symbolized by two lovers before an open fire. The physical fire burning before them is only a distant echo of the fiery passion burning within them.

The fire of divine love is the passionate burning away of all the tangled web of desire and deception that separates us from God. Richard Rolle, the fourteenth-century English mystic, entitled his meditation of Christian transformation *The Fire of Love*.

I felt my heart glow hot and burn. I experienced the burning not in my imagination but in reality, as if it were being done by a physical fire. But I was really amazed by the way the burning heat boiled up in my soul and . . . the unprecedented comfort it brought.[5]

Rolle speaks of how this transforming fire bubbled up from within his heart and melted his hardened shell of self-centeredness. This burning love, "rooted in our hearts and steady in performance, transforms us to His likeness, and He openly pours into us another glory and divine rejoicing." God's love "is fire, making souls fiery, so that they may be shining and burning."[6]

T. S. Eliot draws upon the same storehouse of images that inspired Rolle. Eliot's poem "Little Gidding" develops the contrast between the apocalyptic fires of final destruction and the loving fire of transformation.

> The dove descending breaks the air
> With flame of incandescent terror
> Of which the tongues declare
> The one discharge from sin and error.
> The only hope, or else despair,
>   Lies in the choice of pyre or pyre—
>   To be redeemed from fire by fire.
>
> Who then devised the torment? Love.
> Love is the unfamiliar Name
> Behind the hands that wove
> The intolerable shirt of flame
> Which human power cannot remove.
>   We only live, only suspire,
>   Consumed by either fire or fire.[7]

Fire both purifies and destroys. Our inner fire, our passions and loves, can either purify our hearts or destroy our lives. We are transformed by what we love. We become whatever we desire. We can fix our passions on some object that enhances and completes us. Or we can turn our loves toward an object that fragments and dissipates our wholeness. Somerset Maugham's novel *Of Human Bondage* portrays this conflict movingly. Maugham's protagonist, Philip, is consumed by his desire for a woman that he cannot have and who does not want him. His life is paralyzed by his misdirected love for her.

Our fiery love of Jesus is what transforms us into the image of Christ. The garden tomb is the kiln, fired by the flames of the cross. This transformation is not achieved by our efforts to be like Jesus. Christian transformation involves more than living a good, pious life. Christ must remain the only giver of possibilities for our lives. He is the only source and goal of our passion. Christian transformation is committing our passions to the Christ who dwells at the very center of our lives. The cosmic Word came and dwelt among us so that we could behold its glory. We are given an image, a living, human image, upon whom we can transfer our fragmented and distorted passions.

Our fiery passions no longer need to be scattered among lesser things that shatter and diffuse the wholeness of our lives. Instead, we are given the unifying omega point of all creation. We acquire a single, passionate intentionality in our lives. We no longer scramble madly from one lesser love to the next. Purity of heart, as Kierkegaard called this fiery, passionate love of God, is to will one thing:

> Father in Heaven! What is a man without Thee! What is all that he knows, vast accumulation though it be, but a chipped fragment if he does not know Thee! What is all his striving, could it even encompass the world, but a half-finished work if he does not know Thee: Thee the One, who art one thing and who art all! So may Thou give to the intellect, wisdom to comprehend that one thing; to the heart, sincerity to receive this understanding; to the will, purity that wills only one thing.[8]

Denial of God does not eliminate our need to commit our lives passionately to someone or something. Denial of God only means that our inward fires will be kindled for shadowy illusions rather than something truly life-giving.

Paul develops this concept in the opening chapters of Romans. Human wickedness stems from our passionate love of created things instead of the Creator. As a result, humanity becomes "vain in its imaginations." We exchange the glory of God for images made to look like mortals or even animals. Once our passions are deflected onto these shadows, we are "given over to shameful lusts" (Rom. 1:21-31, NEB).

Christ comes to redeem our misdirected passions and to purify them by turning them back to our Creator. Christ becomes the "image of the invisible God, the first-born of all creation" in whom "God was pleased to dwell" (Col. 1:15-20). Focusing our passions and loves upon Christ, the image of the invisible God, we are transformed by this Christ whom we love. Our passions, which are now directed toward our divine Creator and center, transfigure us back into what we were created to be.

Jesus becomes the true beloved who fans the fires of our passions and directs them toward an authentic center. This accounts for a variety of metaphors found both in the Hebrew Bible and in Christian literature. God's covenant relationship with Israel is spoken of in terms of marriage. Israel is the virgin to whom God is betrothed. Virginity does not refer to sexual status but connotes the singleness of mind with which the lover obeys the beloved. This is contrasted to harlotry in which the people have no single-hearted intentionality but listen to many gods and lovers.[9] Paul employs this same image in his controversy with the church at Corinth. Paul states that he betrothed the church to Christ. The people should show a "sincere and pure devotion." They have, however, readily accepted "another Jesus . . . a different spirit . . . a different gospel" (2 Cor. 11:1ff.).

The Gospels suggest this image in their treatment of John the Baptist and his message. "I baptize you with water for repentance. But after me will come one who is more powerful than I, whose sandals I am not fit to carry. He will baptize you with the Holy Spirit and with fire (Matt. 3:11, NIV). John's coming fire is not just the apocalyptic fire of the endtime. It is also the passionate fire of divine love that Jesus stirs up within those who see and hear him. This is the fire of the Holy Spirit, whose greatest gift is love (1 Cor. 13). The disciples go forth to spread their passionate message of God's love only after the fiery tongues of the Spirit descend upon them.

Both Paul and the Gospels intimate that there is some deep interconnectedness among our passions, our imagination, and personal transformation. When we become vain in our imagination, our passions become disordered. When we direct ourselves toward Christ, the image of the invisible God, our loves attain some purity and singleness of devotion. The human imagination is a complex synthesis of many forces and operations. There are several basic operations that researchers have identified. Through imagination or "phantasy" we project ourselves into future possibilities. Greek *phantastikous* means literally "to represent" or "to make visible." Through our imagination we represent and play out certain possibilities for future action or behavior. Through our imagination we have the "capacity to participate in knowing or performing the act proleptically—that is, trying it on for size, performing it in imagination."[10] Through our capacity to imagine we can create a vision by which we can live. We then try to make real this vision in our lives. The potter performs a similar operation. She envisions a possible form and then tries to create that shape on the wheel or with her hands.

Imagination not only enables us to envision alternative futures for ourselves, it also evokes the energies needed to participate in realizing that future. A third function of imagination is to exert an assimilative influence upon all subsequent perceptual data. Our imaginal system exercises a profound influence upon how we integrate new information into our awareness. That which we cannot imagine possible, we will not see. Even though something is real and standing before us, we might not see it because we cannot imagine its possibility.[11]

God has presented to us a powerful alternative life-vision in Jesus Christ. We are called to make a decision about this vision. We can direct our passions toward it and be tranformed by it. Or we can dismiss it.

Rollo May discusses the role of imagination in his *Love and Will*. When we are informed of certain possibilities, we must then make a decision. Shall we allow ourselves to be formed by them or shall we reject them? Commenting on a passage from Thomas Aquinas, May writes:

> We note the word "being informed" in the passive voice, followed later by form in the active voice. I take this to mean that in the process of knowing, we are informed by the thing understood, and in the same act, our intellect simultaneously gives form to the thing we understand. What is important here is the word "in-form," or "forming in." To tell someone something, to in-form him, is to form him—a process that can sometimes become very powerful in psychotherapy by the therapist's saying just one sentence, or one word, at the right moment.[12]

Through Jesus Christ, God has in-formed us as to what is demanded of us and what possibilities are available to us. God has informed us concerning authentic life. Obediently hearing and seeing this possibility means nothing less than to be formed by it. Since our lives are so distorted and fragmented, this formation is nothing less than a transformation of our lives from being like God to being the image of God. Unless we passionately love God as made known to us in Jesus Christ, we will not look long enough and carefully enough at reality. We will not see what is truly possible.

This is Charles Wesley's point in "Jesus, Thine All-Victorious Love."

> Jesus, thine all-victorious love
> Shed in my heart abroad;
> Then shall my feet no longer rove,
> Rooted and fixed in God.
>
> Refining fire, go through my heart;
> Illuminate my soul;
> Scatter thy life through every part,
> And sanctify the whole.
>
> No longer then my heart shall mourn,
> While purified by grace;
> I only for his glory burn,
> And always see his face.
>
> My steadfast soul, from falling free,
> Shall then no longer move,
> While Christ is all the world to me,
> And all my heart is love.[13]

When we burn only for God's glory, then our lives no longer wobble and rove without center. We are rooted and fixed in God.

Certain disciplines of the Christian life have developed over the centuries that seek to form us through informing us. They seek to keep ever before us the image of Christ. In some ways they inform us of the same truth over and over again. Their intent is to help us grasp the simple shape of the gospel.

Frequently these disciplines have degenerated into extreme acts of asceticism or of self-denial, which only feed our autonomous life projects. In their pure intent, however, they aim to present us again and again with the imaginative possibilities opened up for us in Christ Jesus.

The most important of these disciplines are word and sacrament. When Dietrich Bonhoeffer describes complete obedience to Christ, he includes nothing more than faithful participation in word and sacrament.

> If we would hear his call to follow, we must listen where he is to be found, that is, in the Church through the ministry of Word and Sacrament. The preaching of the Church and the administration of the sacraments is the place where Jesus Christ is present. If you would hear the call of Jesus you need no personal revelation: all you have to do is to hear the sermon and receive the sacrament, that is, to hear the gospel of Christ crucified and risen.[14]

The reformed tradition has always understood that the church is present where the word is faithfully proclaimed and truly heard and where the sacraments are administered according to the institutes of Christ. A Christian people is created where God the center informs them of their possibilities and where they receive new alternatives for their lives.

The Hebrew and Christian scriptures are a storehouse of forgotten alternatives. When we read scripture obediently—so that we truly "hear" it—we are presented with the image of what our lives might become. The gospel is not the pages of the Bible. These simply are the banks which contain and show the direction of the flowing presence of the risen Christ, who moves through time and space as if he were some great river. The Bible keeps us within the boundaries where Christ's presence most powerfully operates.[15] The Bible is the place where God and humanity can peer into each other, sharing a moment or two together. In that moment, scripture flows through us like some ageless wave. Unfortunately, we have lost this sense of scripture. We now spend most of our time not listening to the Bible but rather apologizing for it or defending it.

William Johnston speaks of the transforming quality of holy scripture. He compares Christian biblical approaches to those of Buddhism. Johnston cites a letter that Nichiren, a Buddhist teacher who was devoted to the Lotus Sutra, wrote to his disciple from prison. He tells his friend that if he truly prays the Lotus Sutra with both mind and body, then he will bring salvation to all living creatures. "When some people read the Lotus Sutra, they mouth the words but don't read with the mind. And if they read with the mind, they don't read with the body. To read with both the body and mind is the most exalted."[16] For both Christians and Buddhists the goal is to realize scripture in our lives. In other words, we are to actualize in our lives the possibilities that are presented to our imaginations through scripture.

The pivotal event for many Christians comes when scripture is truly heard. St. Anthony hears Jesus' words to the rich young ruler: Sell all you have, give your possessions to the poor, come and follow me. Anthony takes these words as personally addressed to him and changes the course of Egyptian Christianity. Augustine struggled for years about whether to commit himself to Christianity. One afternoon he was sitting in the garden and heard a voice softly singing to him: Take up and read; take up and read. Nearby was a bound copy of Paul's letters. Snatching it up, he read:

"Not in reveling and drunkenness, not in debauchery and wantonness, not in strife and jealousy. But put on the Lord Jesus Christ." At that moment, Augustine records, "it was as if a light of confidence and security had streamed into my heart, and all the darkness of my former hesitation was dispelled."[17] John Wesley goes reluctantly to a meeting on Aldersgate Street. As Luther's preface to the Book of Romans is read, Wesley feels his heart strangely warmed.

Matthew the Poor is an Egyptian monk who lives in the desert fifty miles southwest of Cairo. Like St. Anthony, Matthew felt that the words of scripture were addressed to him. The prosperous young pharmacist sold his two houses, his cars, his businesses and gave all he had to the poor. From his desert cell, Matthew has directed the total rehabilitation of the ancient monastery of Deir el Makarios and begun a reformation of Coptic monastic life. In 1971 he was one of three nominees for patriarch of the church. He writes of scripture: "God's directions to us are most often given through the reading and hearing of the Gospel, when we are in a state of humility and when we pray with an open heart."[18] Obedience is a spiritual passion that draws us beyond our scattered preoccupations to an encounter with the God who is both the limit and the middle of our lives.

What we hear with our ears in scripture, we see with our eyes in the sacraments. This is particularly true of the Lord's Supper. John 6 records a crisis in Jesus' ministry. The crowds have grown larger and larger, but Jesus senses that the people have come for the wrong reason. They expect to see a miracle-worker or a political liberator. Jesus' discourse is meant to clarify the meaning and nature of his mission. Many followers try to understand what he is saying and then turn away. Raymond Brown has called attention to how this chapter stresses word and sacrament. Jesus' first explanation emphasizes faith, which comes when we hear Jesus' teachings. The church reads the Bible and listens to the word in the first part of its worship. Jesus' second explanation emphasizes his self-sacrifice and death as the means to fullness of life. Similarly, Christians break bread at the foot of the cross after they have heard the word. What is said in scripture is enacted in sacrament. The deepest meanings cannot be spoken but only enacted.[19]

When he breaks the bread and shares the cup, Jesus instructs the disciples to do this for the *anamnesis* of him. The Greek word *anamnesis* has been translated variously as "re-calling," "re-presenting," or "remembering." Our words do not do justice to the full range of *anamnesis*. It is not so much that we remember Jesus who is now absent as we recognize Jesus as presently operative here and now. Jesus is made present again before us. He is re-presented. In the Lord's Supper we take bread and break it. We bless the cup and share it. The one who was the image and likeness of God, the servant obedient unto death, appears to attentive eyes.[20] Those with eyes to see are presented with a new possibility for their own lives. The image of God is restored within them when they accept Jesus' servanthood as the pattern for one's own life. We receive an in-sight, an inner vision, of what our lives might become.

When we eat ordinary bread, we transform it into ourselves. When we eat the bread of life that is Jesus, we transform ourselves into him. William Johnston has assembled several citations from the early church that illustrate this understanding. St. Leo writes in the fifth century that participation in the body and blood of Christ produces in us no other effect than to make us pass into that which we take. Thomas Aquinas taught that when we eat normal food we transform it into ourselves. But in the Eucharist we are transformed into Christ. St. Augustine, whose life was dramatically changed by hearing a word spoken to him, imagines Jesus as saying: "I am the food of the strong; have faith and eat me. But thou wilt not change me into thyself, it is Thou who will be transformed into me."[21]

Christian transformation does not consist of heroic measures and self-imposed acts of denial. It is faithful participation in word and sacrament. If we do only this, we will surely grow. If we do every other spiritual exercise without this, we will only feed our own illusions.

> Our ideal must be, in and for the long run—a genial, gentle, leisurely expansion—no shaking of the nerves, no strain, no semi-physical vehemence, no impatient concentration—suffering and (involuntary) strain may come to us; but all this will, where good, be upborne and expanded into peace and humble power, if we keep little in our own eyes, gently watchful, and united to God in God.[22]

Our most urgent need is to give form to our lives. Centered in ourselves, we lack the store of alternatives and models that provide adequate possibilities for our lives. Sometimes we fail to realize this and use whatever broken fragments we find. Other times we dimly sense our own limitations and look beyond ourselves. Unfortunately we seldom search beyond the nearest object: another person, a nation, a cause. Here also our life project fails. We sputter and lurch our way along the human life cycle, trying to live from the resources of our false center: the images and possibilities for human life that we ourselves can generate.

God, who is both the center and the limit of our

lives, has supplied a way out of this impasse. Jesus Christ offers us a new image and likeness for genuine existence. From this divine center we are informed of the new creation and its possibilities. Presented with the possibility of transformation through our imagination, we must then decide for or against the committing of our lives to its fertile richness.

Applying
The Glaze

The potter is never just an imitator of rocks. A volcano, that demented and blind kiln, spews forth randomly shaped chunks of rock. The potter's kiln, however, is neither blind nor demented. The form conceived by the potter's hands and imagination takes its final shape within the kiln. The potter's creative work, however, is not finished at this point of bisque firing. Now that the pot has been frozen in stone, the potter must decorate it.

The potter decorates her pots. Since the very beginning, potters have adorned their creations with color and design. Decoration can be applied at almost any stage of the clay's development into a pot. It may be as simple as finger impressions on the wet clay. Some of the earliest pots from Syro-Palestine have marks made by rope or matting. The potter sought to imitate woven reed baskets by pressing these natural fibers against the wet clay. Different-colored clays can be mixed to produce a marbled effect in the finished ware. Something as common as a kitchen fork can be used to inscribe the pot's surface.

The two most common forms of decoration are slip and glaze. Slip is a mixture of clay and water that is poured through a sieve and then brushed or sprayed over the clay vessel. Slip trailing uses a technique similar to icing a cake. The slip is trailed from a rubber nozzle over the clay to create a pattern or design. The slip can also be applied to the leather-hard clay and then burnished with a blunt instrument, producing a lustre ware. The sgraffito technique covers the pot with slip and then uses a sharp scriber to scratch through the pigmented slip, revealing the clay body underneath.

Glazing, the other common decorative process, differs from slip in that it does not use a clay-soluble mixture. The clay pot and the glaze do not share a common base. Glazes are a special mixture of silica, flux, and alumina. They adhere to the surface of the clay and then fuse into its body when the pot is fired. Because the glaze is not clay-based, the interaction between the pot and the glaze differs significantly from that of the slip and the pot. A potter can achieve different and striking effects by adding other minerals, oxides, or chemicals to the glaze mixture. The kiln's fire precipitates a chemical exchange between these elements and the clay. Mastering this complex chemical exchange between the dry bisque ware and the glaze is one mark of an accomplished potter.

The bisque firing has dried the clay to a bone-dry state. The clay seems almost to burn with thirst. It seeks something to slake its parched dryness—as if it longs for whatever flows. So long as the clay is still touched by water, it is suspended and impermanent. The same water that wears away the stone also keeps the clay fluid and plastic. Too much water can dissolve the clay back into boundless, formless matter.

When the potter applies the glaze, he is slaking the clay's greedy desire for water. The glaze is a life-giving water because it satisfies the pot's thirst without destroying it. The potter seeks to introduce the glaze's permanent moisture into the very heart of the clay. The second kiln firing will affix the glaze's moisture deep within the clay so that it will thirst no more.

The potter asks the fire not simply to coat the glaze upon the naked clay. The fire is to give the clay a skin of glaze, an epidermis that is permanently moist. Never again will the pot burn with thirst. The glaze firing diffuses the glaze's pigments throughout the clay's mass. It penetrates it much as colored crystals penetrate deep into the stone. The painter applies her oils to the canvas surface. Glazing is a truth of the depths. The glaze enters the very heart of the pot. Its colors transfigure the vessel in unpredictable ways. To select an appropriate glaze is not the same as choosing paint for the kitchen walls at the corner hardware store. I apply a single-tone glaze to a pot. It is speckled after the glaze firing because the glaze's chemicals have reacted to the grit embedded in the clay. In traditional English pottery, the potter always leaves a small strip of the vessel unglazed. Someone who examines the finished pot can thus see how this particular batch of glaze interacted with this unique mixture of clay.

We are not unlike the clay. We also thirst for that which will give us life. We seek something that will satisfy our deepest yearnings. God creates the human heart with a desire for meaning, for loving and being loved. God does this in order that we may reach out and seek our Creator. As surely as we need food and oxygen for survival, we also need God. Psychologist Erik Erikson believes that each child is born with a basic need to trust the world around her as meaningful and caring. This trust is the touchstone of all religion.[1] Our yearning to discover our world as a consistent, dependable, trustworthy reality stirs up within us a desire for an ultimate Provider.

We consume most of our energy trying to discover

objects capable of slaking this yearning. A gnawing sense of being unfulfilled underlies our lives. While occupied with many things, we never feel truly satisfied. The very objects that we hope will end our anxious search often threaten our very existence. We try, by force of our own achievements, to make our world seem dependable and secure. We want to assure that our older years are comfortable by building up sufficient equity. We attempt to secure our social position by manipulation and by domination. We confuse trust with reliability. We assume that if we can make our world behave reliably on our behalf, then it is a trustworthy world. This reliability, however, is the truth of control and prediction. We believe that if only we can control and predict our lives, the lives of others around us, and even the conditions that impact us, then we can satisfy our deepest thirst.

Thus we look everywhere but in the right place. Only at our lives' midpoint do we realize the futility of this approach. In a celebrated and often-cited passage, C. G. Jung states:

> Among all my patients in the second half of life—that is to say, over thirty-five—there has not been one whose problem in the last resort was not that of finding a religious outlook on life. It is safe to say that every one of them fell ill because he had lost that which the living religions of every age have given to their followers, and none of them has been really healed who did not regain his religious outlook.[2]

St. Augustine, long before Jung, made the same observation: "You have made us for Yourself, and our hearts are not at rest, until they rest in you."[3]

One hot, dusty day, Jesus stopped beside a well in Sychar. Asking a Samaritan woman to draw him a drink of water, he tells her that he can give her living water. The woman is perplexed. She does not understand what Jesus means. "Whoever drinks the water that I shall give him will never suffer thirst any more. The water that I shall give him will be an inner spring always welling up for eternal life" (John 4:14, NEB). At the Feast of Tabernacles, a water festival in some of its aspects, Jesus tells the astonished crowds: "If any one thirst, let him come to me and drink. He who believes in me, as the scripture has said, 'Out of his heart shall flow rivers of living water'" (John 7:37-38).

Like dry clay we often seek to quench our thirst for life from springs that do not satisfy. Worse still, even as the clay desires the water that will dissolve it back into the void, we often seek to slake our thirst for life from springs that poison and stunt us. The water that Jesus gives, however, is different.

I recently traveled to southern France, where I stayed in the ecumenical monastery at Taizé. Near the community is an ancient spring that was visited by medieval pilgrims on their way to the Shrine of St. James in Spain. A group of us made a pilgrimage to this spring. We set out from the Church of the Reconciliation and stopped periodically to pray and to meditate. At each stop there would be a rude cross nailed to a tree or set upon a cairn of stones. Sometimes the scripture would be in German; sometimes, in English. Two readings in particular remain with me.

We had stopped in a field, against a low stone wall. The hot August sun was beating down upon us. The heat had turned the pasture grasses brown and brittle. They were dying for lack of water. Coarse straws pricked my hands as I sat down amid the brown grass. Someone read from Isaiah 55:1-3:

Ho, every one who thirsts, come to the waters;
and he who has no money,
   come, buy and eat!
Come, buy wine and milk
   without money and without price.
Why do you spend your money for that
    which is not bread,
   and your labor for that which does not satisfy?
Hearken diligently to me, and eat what is good,
   and delight yourselves in fatness.
 Incline your ear, and come to me;
   hear, that your soul may live.

In the silence that followed the reading, I began to realize that much of my life has been taken up with spending my energy on that which does not satisfy. I live as the dying grass lives. The grass busily sends its roots down into the hard, lifeless dirt, thinking that it will find the life-giving water there. It needs only to lift its eyes upward for the moist, vivifying dew and rain. I was digging and scratching the surface of life. But all I needed to do was to "hear," to incline my ear in obedient trust.

   We came to the spring along a narrow, slippery path that led down a steep escarpment. The spring was nearly hidden beneath the roots of a massive tree which overshadowed it. Someone centuries ago had erected a tunnel of hand-hewn stone that burrowed deep into the cliff. The water was brackish and stagnant as it stood in the dark tunnel. Some dead leaves rested on its bottom, slowly decaying. After prayers and a song, we heard a passage from Revelation 7:15–17:

Therefore are they before the throne of God,
   and serve him day and night within his temple;
   and he who sits upon the throne

will shelter them with his presence.
They shall hunger no more, neither thirst any more;
  the sun shall not strike them,
    nor any scorching heat.
For the Lamb in the midst of the throne
    will be their shepherd,
  and he will guide them to springs of living water;
and God will wipe away every tear from their eyes.

Our guide left us. We were free to remain at the spring as long as we wished. We could respond to the water in any way that seemed right for us. Some of us dipped our hands into the pool. Others bent down and washed their faces. Still others cupped their hands and dipped some water from the pool, drinking it slowly and reverently.

I sat there a long time. I thought about the generations who had stopped here. I thought about their faith and devotion. I thought about my inner thirst for meaning. I felt an intense urge to respond physically to this sacred spring and to its water. I wanted to kneel and to drink. Yet the idea was repugnant to me. *Don't drink the water in Europe,* said my inner voice, although I knew that it was a precaution from an earlier age. This water, however, looked unhealthy. It was brackish and unappealing. No matter where I found such water, I would not want to drink it. My will was conflicted. I broke the impasse by a sudden gesture. I cupped my hands and drank. To my surprise the water was cool and refreshing. It tasted clean and pure.

Is this how it is with the living water that God gives? The springs that look appealing to us will never satisfy. They seduce us with their lovely promises of vitality through control and success. These sources are not only false, they are also dangerous. They will ultimately dissolve us back into the void. The living water, the glaze that would permanently enter our dry lives and slake our desires, seldom appears attractive or life-giving. It takes an act of decision, an overriding of our natural instincts, to drink this living water. Is this the opaqueness of God? God's gracious self-giving is not where we expect it to be.

This is certainly the affirmation of Second Isaiah: "Truly, thou art a God who hidest thyself, O God of Israel, the Savior" (Isa. 45:15). Repeatedly the psalmists cry out to God, "Why do you hide yourself?" (See Psalms 10:1; 13:1; 44:24; 88:14.) One of Martin Luther's favorite expressions was "the hidden God." We do not expect God to be found in a man who hangs on a cross. We do not look for God in an act of self-surrender that feels as if it were death itself. Yet this is where the hidden God resides. Only those who hear attentively and obediently can perceive the truth.

We, of course, go to the nearest and most obvious sources in order to slake our thirst for wholeness and meaning. The real source of our lives is hidden from us. Only obedience as the attentive listening to and seeing of life's depths can reveal it. This spring is never obvious because it bubbles forth from the wounded body of Christ. "One of the soldiers stabbed his side with a lance, and at once there was a flow of blood and water" (John 19:34, NEB).

The clay must pass through fire in order for the glaze to penetrate its depths. The kiln's high temperatures soften the clay so that it melts slightly. In this semi-liquid state, the glaze's permanent moisture enters into it. Unless the pot passes through the fire, nothing has changed. A potter can dip a bisque-fired pot into the glaze and then, deciding that another glaze is more suitable, wash it off under the water faucet. Only fire makes the glaze permeate the clay.

Neither can we put on Christ without passage

through fire. This ordeal by fire is part of God's hiddenness. It is also why that which gives us life appears as life-threatening. We must pass through ordeal by fire. In Par Lagerkvist's novel there is a scene in which the two prisoners, Barabbas and the prisoner to whom he is chained, Sahak, are observed praying by their foreman. The foreman asserts that he is a prudent man who takes no chances. He prays and sacrifices to many gods in order to cover all his bets. He wants to know the name of Sahak's god. Sahak replies that the crucified God demands no sacrifices. Instead Christ requires only that one sacrifice oneself.

> What's that you say? Sacrifice oneself? What do you mean?
> Well, that one sacrifice oneself in his great smelting furnace, Sahak said.
> In his smelting-furnace . . .[4]

We must face a transformative diminishment. Our self-centered ego must suffer diminution in order to rest within the divine center. Our conformity to the cross resets our fragmented awareness into a greater whole. This is not suffering for the sake of pain and punishment. It is our reintegration into wholeness. Teilhard de Chardin speaks of God's hands that lovingly work the clay of life. God's gentle and mighty hands reach down into our souls. "Into these hands it is comforting to surrender oneself."[5]

> Through everything in me that has subsistence and resonance, everything that enlarges me from within, everything that arouses me, attracts me, wounds me from without; through all these, Lord, you work upon me, you mold and spiritualize my formless clay, you transform me into yourself . . . . and I am conscious

of bearing deep within me all the strain and struggle of the universe.[6]

The person that I might be is not limited to the individual that I am. I will never discover my person-hood in its totality unless I suffer a diminishment of my own center, unless I take the tremendous risk of surrendering my partial vision. Such surrender is always painful because it feels as if something is dying. Our partial, truncated self, which sees only the ground and not the field, must be integrated into some larger wholeness. It is dethroned and diminished. It no longer occupies the center. Now, however, its life can flow from the center. Ordeal by fire is ultimately a process of fusion, not disintegration.

I remember the first pot that I made. It was a pinch pot. I had added a short foot to the bottom of it so that it stood about two inches above the ground. I was almost embarrassed when I looked at it. It was lumpy and ill-conceived. The rim undulated erratically. I thought to myself, *If this is the best that I can do, then I had better look for another craft to learn.* My next few pots were not much better. I looked at them on the drying shelf with a bit of discouragement. *Nothing I do to these,* I thought, *will make them look anything but ugly.*

One day it was time to glaze them. I looked at the various tubs of glaze that were stacked in one corner of the workshop. Their labels, defining them by their chemical contents, told me very little about how they would look on my ugly ducklings. Above the tubs was a chart. Small glazed tiles showed how the different glazes would look on a fired pot. I couldn't believe that any of them would look good on my poor pots. I took the course of least resistance and randomly dipped each pot in a different tub.

A few days later, I went into the kiln room. I

searched the cluttered shelves and looked for my pots. I looked on the upper shelves. I looked below. I shoved the pots in the front to one side and peered toward the back of each shelf. I could not find my pots. *Perhaps,* I thought, *they even felt ugly and self-destructed in the kiln.* Finally I located them. I knew they were mine because my initials were scratched on their bottoms. I had not discovered them earlier because they were much more attractive than I had dreamed they could be.

The glaze had filled the rough spots and smoothed out the lumps. The play of color and light made even the uncertain and graceless lines look lovely. This is transformation in Christ.

> In these you once walked, when you lived in them. But now put them all away: anger, wrath, malice, slander, and foul talk from your mouth. Do not lie to one another, seeing that you have put off the old nature with its practices and have put on the new nature, which is being renewed in knowledge after the image of its creator.
> —Colossians 3:7-10

Our perishable nature must put on the imperishable. Our mortal nature must put on the immortal. We have borne the image of Adam and Eve, the man and woman of dust. Now we must bear the image of Christ, the heavenly one. Our lives are distorted and barren, as if they were the dry bisque ware produced by a beginning potter. When we put on Christ, we allow the beautiful glaze of the new creation to penetrate our dusty, dry lives. Christ breaks through our hard shell of resistance and plumbs the depths of our being. The beauty of Christ's life crystallizes within us, even as the bits of glaze fuse not just with the surface clay but also with the pot's inner body.

Christ's life sparkles from the profundity of our being even as the quartz and mica glitter within the dark granite. God's grace and the potter's glaze achieve much the same effect. God, the cosmic potter, covers us with the glaze of Christ. This divine glaze not only satisfies our deepest thirst but transforms our very nature. We no longer bear the imprint of the man and woman of dust but are covered with the beauty of Christ.

Grace is God's energetic process of changing us into the likeness of Jesus Christ. God's grace breaks through our crusty outer covering and mingles with our given human qualities. Grace is not something set over against human nature, as if to annul and to destroy it. It is meant to mingle with our natures and to restore them to their original state. In Christ what was once ours by nature is restored by grace.

The glaze does not burn through the clay and dissolve it, leaving only a fragile web of glaze with nothing to support it. Neither does grace destroy our humanity. It transforms us into the image of the new creation in the same way that the glaze penetrates and transforms the raw bisque ware. Everything changes, but everything remains the same. Once again we encounter the paradoxical nature of Christian faith.

Anthony de Mello quotes a haiku poem from Japan:

> Oh wondrous marvel:
> I chop wood!
> I draw water from the well!

De Mello then observes that for most people there is nothing wonderful about drawing water or chopping wood. Those who have received enlightenment, however, see wonder in even the most prosaic activities. "After enlightenment nothing really changes

. . . There's one major difference: now you see all of these things with a different eye."[7] Grace transfigures, but does not destroy, all the other components of our basic human equipment. An approach to Christian transformation that speaks of destroying the flesh, killing the self, or abolishing our human nature is a dangerous and destructive spirituality. Grace transfigures; it never destroys.

This transfiguration of the human personality, de Mello suggests, has something to do with how we perceive the world. Biologists and other researchers have discovered that the human eye and mind are capable of perceiving either the field or the ground but never both at once. We look at the tree and see the row of houses as background. Or we look at the row of houses and see the tree as foreground. But we cannot fix our eyes on both images simultaneously. We look into the picture puzzle and see the urn or the two faces looking at each other. But we cannot see the urn and the faces at the same time. As long as we live under the power of the old creation, in which we attempt to live at our own center, we perceive the world incorrectly. Presented with a complex picture of reality, we make the wrong selection between the field and the ground. We see a part rather than the whole. Christian transformation is when we look at the picture but see it differently.

The ego's self-centered vision is not entirely bad. There are times when we need to look at the world through the lens of our own center. Without a strong self-identity, psychologists tell us, we would have no sense of separation between ourselves and our world. We would end up as either autistic or psychotic. The self-centered ego is only "bad" because it is too limited and partial. It leaves out too much of the picture. It is too restrictive. The world we experience is a much bigger place than our ego ever lets us know. It defends us from harm and caters to our needs, but sometimes it is overly protective. It prevents us from experiencing the fullness of life. There are times when it is important to discriminate between the field and the ground. There are other times when we need to experience both of them. If the limited ego-perception is the only lens through which we perceive reality, our lives are impoverished. In Christopher Fry's *The Firstborn*, Moses tells the pharaoh:

> A man has more to be
> Than a Pharaoh. He must dare to outgrow the se-
>   curity
> Of partial blindness.[8]

Christian transformation does not abolish our ego and its awareness. It is too important for our human functioning and surviving. Grace instead penetrates this dimension with a more profound awareness. It transcends our normal perception insofar as it allows us to see reality as both the urn and the faces simultaneously. Everything remains the same, yet everything changes.

Were Christian transformation to destroy our basic sense of self, which is part of the fundamental human equipment, it would render us helpless and incapable of action. Grace does not destroy the "flesh" anymore than the glaze destroys the pot.

Paul tells the church at Corinth: "Our desire is to have the new body put on over it, so that our mortal part may be absorbed into life immortal. God himself has shaped us for this very end" (2 Cor. 5:4-5, NEB). Paul does not say that the mortal is to be destroyed. The Spirit's action enables the immortal to penetrate the mortal. Nothing is destroyed. Everything is transfigured. We perceive our personal reality in a new way. This mutual interpenetration of mortal and immortal generates within us the capacity to see the shimmering stream of life that flows through all reality. God's uncreated energies flow eternally from the divine center into the midst of our material world. They infuse new possibilities and new occasions of experience. Only transfigured personalities, however, can comprehend this flow and participate in it.

C H A P T E R 7

Evaluating The Finished Product

I place the glazed pot on my desk. Many weeks have passed since I first tugged at the raw clay in the barrel and tore off a chunk for wedging. Pottery is not a craft for those in a hurry. It takes time. It requires patience. I act and shape reality; but weeks, perhaps even months, must pass before I can see the finished work and evaluate it.

All along the way, the ultimate realization remains just beyond my control. It is my task to build the pot, but I cannot control the results. I do everything that it is possible for me to do. Yet many things can go wrong at every step. The air in the room may be too dry and crack my pot while it air-dries. There may be a small pebble or piece of sponge embedded in the clay. When I trim the footring or cut a decoration into the pot, I pull the hidden intruder from the clay, leaving a gaping hole that I cannot repair. The firing reveals and tests my craft. It uncovers all the hidden flaws. An air bubble that I missed during the wedging may explode the pot's wall. A handle or lug that I attached to the vessel's main body may not have joined properly. When the kiln temperature rises, the joint cracks and separates. Certain forms cannot hold weight as the clay softens during firing. An angle that I saw as graceful may lack strength and collapse as the clay softens. The glaze may blister from the heat. I may have held the pot under the glaze for a moment too long. The extra thickness of glaze then "crawls" when it is fired. Hairline cracks craze across the surface. I select a particular glaze coloring for this pot. The kiln's mixture of air and heat causes a different chemical reaction and the color is entirely different. Sometimes just the location of the pot in the kiln can affect the pot's glazing. One near the kiln wall will become hotter than a vessel near its center. Two pots, dipped in the same glaze, will have a different surface because one of them was nearer the kiln wall. A thousand little, unpredictable events can alter all my envisioned designs.

I can only surrender my efforts to the ceramic process. I can cooperate with these even as they remain independent of me. I do everything possible to assure positive results. I cannot, however, burst into flame and transmute the soft, moist clay into stoneware. I cannot step into the 2300° F kiln and touch up the glaze.

I have been engaged in the concentration of energy since I first wedged the stiff and resistant clay. The totality of my gestures remains both a mystery and a surprise to me. I intervene at the heart of matter to give it another shape, which I have preformed in my imagination. The final translation of this inner image eludes my power. Fire is the only thing we know that is both hard to ignite and difficult to put out. It remains independent of our control while it cooperates with our requests. It is both the birthday candles that continue to burn after we have blown them out and the wood stove that refuses to light.

So I live in tension: How will it look? Will it survive? Will my effort have been worth it? So much time passes between the hand that reaches into the barrel of raw clay and the hand that pulls the finished, glazed pot from the kiln that it requires patience and tenacity to see the process through to its completion. The vessel's initial form is built up rapidly from the felt dialogue among the hands, the eyes, and the imagination. The final judgment on this creation lies beyond all of them. The inconsistency and unpredictability of the ceramic process alone determine the vessel's destiny.

In Luke 14:28-33, Jesus advises his disciples to count the cost before they undertake the cross of discipleship. I cannot anticipate how the vision that I imagined as this particular bowl will appear when I take it from the kiln. How, then, can I ever predict the cost of discipleship? Can I really predict what it means to take up the cross and follow Jesus? Even my most convinced actions are only gestures and questions. My very existence is both figuratively and literally beyond my conception, even as the finished pot's existence lies beyond the potter's conception of it.

So we are left with a tension. Our most convinced actions are only questions. We respond to this tension in one of two ways. We can deny it and throw ourselves frantically into the business of grasping and controlling our lives. Or we can accept our limits and learn to cooperate with those forces beyond us. Most of us prefer the route of denial. We manipulate. We cling. We clutch.

This is the reaction of Promethean humanity. Prometheus, according to Greek mythology, stole fire from the gods and gave it to humankind. What the gods will not give to us we will snatch from them. We will wrest control from God and possess it for ourselves. In despair of God's gracious care, unable to trust that our actions will be gathered into some meaningful pattern, we create for ourselves the sign, the value, that we fear God will refuse to give.

In pride, in reas'ning pride, our error lies;
All quit their sphere, and rush into the skies.
Pride still is aiming at the blest abodes,
Men would be angels, angels would be gods.[1]

We gradually fall into the familiar dynamics of ego-centeredness: functional self-sufficiency, a one-sided emphasis on security, isolation from vital sharing, and the inability to admit vulnerability on any level.

Such clutching and controlling is self-destructive. It accomplishes exactly the opposite of what we hope to attain through it. The potter who tried to control the fire's effect upon her pots would perish amid the kiln's flames. Moses, in *The Firstborn*, tells his nephew Shendi that the dream of power and success is a dangerous one.

Make yourself live, then, Shendi;
But be sure it is life. The golden bear Success
Hugs a man close to its heart; and breaks his bones.
We come upon ourselves, as though we were chance,
Often by the most unwilling decisions
Our maturities hid themselves from our wishes.
And when at last we touch our natures into life
Is at that drastic angle of experience
Where we divide from our natures.[2]

Our thirst for self-achievement and for control of our life project is self-defeating. The desire to succeed is the real author of failure. To try to control the success of the ceramic process is to be paralyzed. To be paralyzed is to fail. I become an observer of myself. I am so self-conscious of what I am doing and how it might turn out later that I cannot give myself over to doing what I must do in the here and now. We become so engrossed in observing ourselves that we cannot give our full attention to the tasks immediately before us. We cannot live creatively because we are absorbed in our own act of creating.

Sports commentators will sometimes speak of how a close game is lost because one player or the whole team "tensed up." They became so self-critical that they could not play naturally and spontaneously. They beat themselves by being too absorbed in how they were playing. They were watching themselves play instead of playing.

W. Timothy Galloway describes a different approach to playing tennis in *The Zen of Tennis*. Most tennis teachers, Galloway says, use a method that gives many instructions about how the player should hold his or her body. Don't bend your arm. Bend your arm. Lower your backswing. Raise your backswing. Tighten your grip. Loosen your grip. Soon the players are so involved in sensing what their bodies are doing that they cannot watch the ball and hit it. Galloway developed a method of teaching that just asks the student to try to hit the ball as effectively as possible without concentrating on where his feet are, whether his swing follows through, or any of the other usual concerns. He teaches the student not to criticize himself or herself. He encourages the students to observe what they are doing and how they are doing it, but they must not evaluate whether it is good or bad at that moment. There is a time for evaluation, but it is later. They should develop a sense of detachment about their performance. They lock themselves into being poor players when they criticize themselves for not doing this or doing that. The energy that should go into the game is then dissipated on observing themselves.

When I was learning to throw a pot on the wheel, I had great difficulty centering the clay. I would concentrate on the way that my hands interlocked. I would focus my mind on my hands and place them as nearly as I could into the position that I had seen in the manuals and the way my teacher had shown me. I could not, however, center the clay. Concentrating on how my hands were held, I made my fingers stiff and my arms tense. I communicated this tension to the clay. When I would feel the clay moving onto center, I would tense up a bit more, thinking, *Now this is how I must hold my right hand*. My nervous concentration would then nudge the clay back off its center.

Later I had the same problem when I was learning how to trim the pot's rim. As the walls rise upward, they become uneven. Not all the clay distributes itself in the same way around the rim. In order to have a cylinder or bowl with an even and level top, the excess clay must be trimmed. As the pot spins rapidly, the potter presses a needle into the whirling walls and lets it slowly cut through the clay. It is important to hold the needle level, otherwise a ragged and uneven cut will be made. Once the needle has cut through the clay, then, with a quick and smooth gesture, the potter lifts the trimmed clay away from the pot. It looks easy enough. I found it incredibly difficult. I would concentrate on keeping my hand level and become more aware of my hand than the needle. The more I worried about the needle slipping, the more tense my hand became. The more tense I was, the more sure I was to slip. When I tried to lift the trimmed clay from the revolving wheel, I would concentrate on my hands rather than on the spinning clay. Almost inevitably I would damage the pot as I lifted the clay away from it. Some days I would keep trimming and retrimming until no walls were left.

When I became too self-critical, I would tense up and my movements would become jerky and unnatural. I could relax and center the clay or trim the pot only when I no longer evaluated my gestures in the midst of doing them. The energy I had consumed in self-criticism could then be directed to the task.

We defeat ourselves when we become self-critical. We experience both liberation and renewed vigor when we do the best that we can while entrusting the results to a power beyond us. This is the second and more mature response to our human limitations. Second Isaiah mocks the Babylonians for their worship of idols.

> Listen to me, house of Jacob
> and all the remnant of the house of Israel,
> a load on me from your birth,
>   carried by me from the womb:
>   till you grow old I am He,
> and when white hairs come, I will carry you still;
> I have made you and I will bear the burden,
>   I will carry you and bring you to safety,
>   To whom will you liken me? Who is my equal?
>   With whom can you compare me? Where is my
>   like?
>   Those who squander their bags of gold
> and weigh out their silver with a balance
> hire a goldsmith to fashion them into a god;
>   then they worship it and fall prostrate before it;
> they hoist it shoulder-high and carry it home;
>   they set it down on its base;
>   there it must stand, it cannot stir from its place.
>   Let a man cry to it as he will, it never answers him;
>   it cannot deliver him from his troubles.
>   —Isaiah 46:3–7, NEB

Second Isaiah contrasts the Babylonians, who carry their idols upon their backs, with Israel's God, who carries the people. While the Babylonians are exhausted by the burden they must carry, Israel experiences the creative vigor that comes from knowing one's efforts are buoyed up by some greater power. Our proud self-images can become idols of control and power that consume our personal energy. We then have nothing left for the tasks that truly need to be done. This is not the case with those who trust in God and know that the meaning and value of their lives do not rest on their own efforts. They know that God carries them and that they do not have to carry God.

Jesus makes this point in Matthew's Sermon on the Mount. "Do not be anxious about tomorrow, for tomorrow will be anxious for itself. Let the day's own trouble be sufficient for the day" (Matt. 6:34). Jesus also told his disciples not to be observers of their own acts of charity and devotion: Don't say your prayers on the streetcorner but go into your closet. Don't make a display of fasting but do it secretly. Never let your right hand know what the left is doing.

We can become so engrossed in observing ourselves that we cannot act freely and with the sort of abandonment that creative living demands. If we turn ourselves into observers of our own prayers, trying to anticipate and to control our emotions as well as to shape God's response, then we are giving a show for our own benefit. We may enjoy ourselves and what we are doing. We are at one and the same time praying and listening. Not being content to wait for God's answer, we provide our own answer. Jesus warns against the danger of praying in the marketplace and on the streetcorner. We can fill our closet with just as many inner spectators as could ever watch us on the streetcorner.

The results of our Christian discipleship lie beyond our control. When we take up our cross and follow Jesus, we can predict neither where it will take us nor what we will accomplish. Jesus said to Peter: "When you were young you fastened your belt about you and

121

walked where you chose; but when you are old you will stretch out your arms, and a stranger will bind you fast, and carry you where you have no wish to go (John 21:18 (NEB). Like the potter who unself-consciously throws and fires his pots, the disciple does the task at hand and lets go of it. She observes what she is doing and feeling, but she does not become overly self-critical.

Christian disciples can do this because they know that their actions are carried by One who is stronger than they are. We need not be anxious about our performance because we can trust the One who guides the totality of our gestures. John Wesley's covenant prayer states beautifully this balance between responsibility and detachment.

> I am no longer my own, but thine. Put me to what thou wilt, rank me with whom thou wilt; put me to doing, put me to suffering; let me be employed for thee or laid aside for thee, exalted for thee or brought low for thee; let me be full, let me be empty; let me have all things, let me have nothing: I freely and heartily yield all things to thy pleasure and disposal.[3]

We yield all we do and all we are to God, but we do not predetermine how God will utilize those gifts that we share. We may be employed or we may be laid aside.

This, however, is a far cry from sitting back and doing nothing. Sometimes the slogan "Let Go and Let God" becomes an excuse to abdicate our God-entrusted responsibilities. Genuine "letting go and letting God" includes doing our tasks as effectively and as responsibly as we can, yet never attempting to predict or to control the results. We do our best without evaluating our performance. Abandonment to the will of God is passionately active and infinitely passive. Jean-Pierre de Caussade, writing during the early eighteenth century to his spiritual directees, told them not to be anxious about what they were or were not doing. They should merely do what lies before them.

> Leave everything else to God, except for your love and obedience to the duties of the present moment . . . The instant response to our immediate duties is, of course, also action. It is the action by which we fulfill God's will made apparent to us by external situations and events . . . . we must be active in all that the present moment demands of us, but in everything else remain passive and abandoned and do nothing but peacefully await the promptings of God.[4]

Christian maturity can be gauged from the capacity to balance control with letting go. We must learn when to be active and when to be passive. This entails a detachment from the strengths and weaknesses of our own accomplishments. We need not repudiate what we have done. Neither do we cling to it for our sense of worth and value. "Either the soul congratulates itself upon its success, and is lifted up; or it is distressed over its failure, and is utterly cast down . . . . in the life of trust neither will trouble us," writes Hannah Whitall Smith. Having committed ourselves in our work to the Lord, "we shall be satisfied to leave it to Him, and shall not think about ourselves in the matter at all."[5]

This alternation between activity and passivity, engagement and detachment, is part of a larger rhythm of life. Listen to your heart pumping. Within our bodies we can hear the alternation between the diastole of rest and the systole of action. I lift a pot from the kiln and a whole complex interaction occurs in my body. Some muscles tighten while others relax. I kick the flywheel and send the clay spinning. Each kick involves two muscular actions. The adductor contracts and the extensor lets go. The key to effective living is to know when to act and when to remain passive. The Christian insight is that we act in the present and release both the past and the future.

Paul, writing to the church at Rome, suggests that this is the function of the Spirit. Each member of the church, Paul writes, is to live according to the spiritual gifts that God has given to them. They are not to be concerned about how their deeds compare to those of their brothers and sisters. They are to concern themselves only with their given task. "By the grace given to me I bid every one among you not to think of himself more highly than he ought to think . . . . For as in one body we have many members, and all the members do not have the same function, so we, though many, are one body in Christ" (Rom. 12:3-5).

Jesus sends his disciples out to the villages and towns of Judah. He tells them not to worry about the results they might achieve. They are not to try to control how other people respond to them. They are not to become self-critical about their performance. "And if any one will not receive you or listen to your words, shake off the dust from your feet as you leave that house or town" (Matt. 10:14). Focus upon the task entrusted to you. Do not be concerned about what you did previously or about how what you are doing now will shape your future. The Spirit will enable you to perform adequately whatever task you carry. You do not have to bear it by yourself.

> You will be dragged before governors and kings for my sake, to bear testimony before them and the Gentiles. When they deliver you up, do not be anxious

how you are to speak or what you are to say; for what you are to say will be given to you in that hour; for it is not you who speak, but the Spirit of your Father speaking through you.

—Matthew 10:18-20

The potter learns very quickly that he cannot waste precious time and energy trying to control what the future will do to his work. He can only give his fullest attention to the work before him. The moment his attention strays to the past or the future, he is distracted from what he must do in the present. Following Jesus demands of us this same balancing of activity and passivity. We are to plunge with all our powers and abilities into the midst of our given tasks. We do them as competently as we possibly can. We must resist through the power of the Spirit any temptation to evaluate or to categorize our failures and achievements.

Fare forward, you who think that you are voyaging;
You are not those who saw the harbour
Receding, or those who will disembark.
Here between the hither and the farther shore
While time is withdrawn, consider the future
And the past with an equal mind.
At the moment which is not of action or inaction
You can receive this: 'on whatever sphere of being
The mind of a man may be intent
At the time of death'—that is the one action
(And the time of death is every moment)
Which shall fructify in the lives of others:
And do not think of the fruit of action.
Fare forward.[6]

Caring
For the Creation

One of the most beautiful and detailed descriptions of a potter at work is in the Bible. Ben Sirach contrasts the responsibilities of the scholar with the common labor of tradespeople and craftspeople. Ben Sirach cannot believe that those who work with their hands can attain wisdom. This belief is not limited to Ben Sirach. The leisured and well-educated have shared this conviction in almost every age. He writes:

> How can the plowman become wise . . . ?
> His mind is fixed on the furrows he traces,
>   and his evenings pass in fattening his heifers.
> So it is with every worker and craftsman,
>   toiling day and night;
> those who engrave seals,
>   always trying to think of new designs:
> they set their heart on producing a good likeness
>   and stay up perfecting the work.
> . . . .
> So it is with the potter, sitting at his work,
>   turning the wheel with his feet;
> constantly on the alert over his work,
>   each flick of the finger premeditated;
> he pummels the clay with his arm,
>   and puddles it with his feet;

he sets his heart on perfecting the glaze,
and stays up cleaning the kiln.
All these put their trust in their hands,
and each is skilled at his own craft.
. . . .
They are not remarkable for culture or sound judg-
ment,
and are not found among the inventors of maxims.
But they give solidity to the created world,
while their prayer is concerned with what pertains
to their trade.
—Ecclesiasticus 38:25-39, JB

Ben Sirach is suggesting that those who ramble through libraries or sit in seats of power are the heartbeat of a culture. They make the decisions that shape social and political life. The common folk, on the other hand, have little to contribute.

Working with their hands in dirt and mud, potters had no place in polite society. They were aliens in their own land throughout most of the ancient world. Potters and other artisans in ancient Athens were aliens with no citizenship rights.[1] The same situation probably prevailed in Israel. The Kenites, who worked as smiths in ancient Israel, were nomadic groups. They were "tent-dwellers" who had no permanent citizenship (Judg. 4:11; 5:24). We may assume that this situation characterized other craftspeople, including potters. In First Chronicles 4:23, the potters belong to their separate guild.

Potters may have been regarded as outside the acceptable culture merely because of where they worked. Jeremiah 19:2 mentions a Potsherd Gate that led from Jerusalem to the Hinnom Valley. Jerusalem's potters worked in the vicinity of this gate. The Hinnom Valley would have been an ideal place for potteries. Water ran in the valley during the winter. The Pool of

Siloam would have been just a short distance away during the summer. Since water is an essential lubricant during the throwing of pots, this would have been an important factor. The Hinnom Valley also had a bad reputation. Kings, Chronicles, and Jeremiah repeatedly mention that this area was the site for child sacrifices to alien gods (2 Kings 23:10; 2 Chron. 28:3; Jer. 32:35). The memory of these cults of child sacrifice in the Hinnom Valley also shaped the New Testament concept of hell. Gehenna (Matt. 5:22) is a Greek transcription of the Hebrew *gi' hennom*, Hinnom Valley. In this same area is the potter's field that was bought with Judas' money as a burial ground for paupers. Pottery was a common task. Its practitioners had no status.

There is, then, great irony in Ben Sirach's observations. This snobbish court intellectual actually pays potters a compliment without intending to do so. The common folk, he observes, go about their daily tasks with love and care. The potter does not spin out elegant speculations about the meaning of life. The potter lives life. The potter does not engage in philosophical reflections about God. He prays to God about the most humble, daily concerns. The potter merely trusts his hands. The potter does the simple task that must be done for any civilization to survive. He is not at the bottom of the social structure. He is its indispensible base. He gives reality its substance and continuity. The common, everyday work of our hands is what truly makes us human.

This is quite true on a practical level. Empires rise and fall; but potters, farmers, and blacksmiths go about their tasks in an ageless way. They preserve human continuity across cultural and political upheaval. Thomas Hardy observed the agricultural crisis of England during the late nineteenth century and wrote "In Time of 'The Breaking of Nations.'"

> Only a man harrowing clods
>   In a slow silent walk
> With an old horse that stumbles and nods
>   Half asleep as they stalk.
>
> Only thin smoke without flame
>   From the heaps of couch-grass;
> Yet this will go onward the same
>   Though Dynasties pass.[2]

Farmers, potters, and others who work with their hands and bodies go on maintaining the continuity of human life while empires rise and fall.

Pottery is also not a cumulative discipline. A beginner does not pick up the craft where the previous generation left it. She does not inherit a certain set understanding of how pottery must be done. She must go back to the very beginning. She must recapitulate in her own experience the total evolution of her art. When she picks up her first lump of raw clay and molds it in her hands, she has no advantage over the Neolithic woman who smeared the first clay over her reed basket in some now-vanished Anatolian village. As the beginner learns and grows, she gains some insight into the evolution of human culture and discipline.

There is also a less obvious spiritual meaning to Ben Sirach's comment. This dimension arises out of the material craft of pottery. As I turn the clay cylinder on my wheel, I touch the clay only at the one point where it glides between my fingers. Yet I am shaping the whole pot. The clay shifts, rises, spreads, contracts in response to that single point. We can experience the whole of reality if we can truly touch it even at one single point. When we immerse ourselves in the small and sometimes boring daily tasks, we touch not merely the surface of life but its depths. Unfortunately, we often miss this encounter. We, along with Ben Sirach, assume that meaning is a matter of the mind and not of the hands. We expect to think great thoughts in our minds rather than to touch truth with our hands. Jean-Pierre de Caussade believes that

> to adore Jesus on Thabor, or to accept the will of God expressed through remarkable circumstances, does not prove that our faith is stronger or better than to accept gladly God's will in the petty affairs of life . . . . To discover God just as clearly in very minor or ordinary things as in the big things of life, is to have a far from normal faith. It is one that is great and extraordinary.[3]

De Caussade reminds us that we can only think and feel with our bodies. Truth is only truth when it is felt with the hands.

Our modern culture, especially American culture, has pursued a radical separation of mind and body. When the life of the mind is separated from the rest of creation, it turns destructively on the world and ultimately on itself. At the beginning of our modern era, Shakespeare spoke of this.

> Poor soul, the center of my sinful earth,
> Lord of these rebel powers that thee array,
> Why dost thou pine within and suffer dearth,
> Painting thy outward walls so costly gay?
> Why so large cost, having so short a lease,
> Dost thou upon thy fading mansion spend?
> Shall worms, inheritors of this excess,

Eat up thy charge? is this thy body's end?
Then, soul, live thou upon thy servant's loss,
And let that pine to aggravate thy store;
Buy terms divine in selling hours of dross;
Within be fed, without be rich no more:
So shalt thou feed on death, that feeds on men,
And death once dead, there's no more dying then.[4]

The mind separates itself from the body and tries to live the divine life in this passing world. The cost is very high: the body must be condemned to hours of dross.

Our social stratification is based on this same division. To work with our hands is nothing but empty dross. Those who work with their bodies are considered uncultured. "Office workers" who work with their minds are somehow a better kind of people. The farmer's son does not think to better himself by becoming a better farmer than his parents. He improves himself by learning a better profession. The potter's daughter does not think of becoming a better potter. She dreams of becoming an art teacher. Richard Jeffries created during the 1880s a style of prose narrative that we now call the "country diary" or the "country journal." Yet Jeffries fled from his own farm home as soon as possible and as an adult lived in cities. His earlier essays reveal the modern mind's contempt for the body's hours of dross. He portrays the Wiltshire agricultural worker in the worst light possible.

For all the conditions and circumstances of such a life tend to one end only—the blunting of all the finer feelings, the total erasure of sensitiveness. The coarse, half-cooked cabbage, the small bit of fat . . . . The man grows insensible to the weather, so cold and damp; his bodily frame becomes crusted over, case-

131

hardened; and with this indifference there rises up at the same time a corresponding dullness as regards all moral and social matters.[5]

We dream of escaping from bodily labor. What we value are leisure, fashion, and etiquette. Vacations are the stepchild of our modern world.

The result of this separation of mind and body is disease. Modern civilization's creativity has degenerated into mere production. The potter turns one pot at a time and invests herself totally in that single creation. The cement plant can produce thousands of bricks each hour. We lose all sense of perspective. Our connection with the flesh and blood of nature grows weaker and weaker. We recklessly build up urban environments that we cannot maintain and see them slowly subside into rubble. We create new products that are meant to increase our leisure time. We crave labor-saving devices so that we can frantically run about looking for something new to do. There is a kind of madness to a society that is preoccupied with automobiles, elevators, and other machines that save us from physical exertion but that then spends millions of dollars on jogging shoes and exercise books.

Good work is not drudgery; it is connective. I touch the spinning clay at only one point, but I feel the whole pot move through my fingers. I feel truth with my body. "Such work is unifying, healing . . . It defines us as we are: not too good to work with our bodies, but too good to work poorly or joylessly or selfishly or alone.[6]

To say that we feel truth with our bodies is another way of saying that work is a sacrament. Good work has a redemptive quality to it. There is a Chinese legend of a noble who is riding through a village. He sees a potter at work. Admiring the finished pots, the noble dismounts and speaks with the potter. "How," he asks, "are you able to form these vessels so that they possess such beauty?" The potter answers, "You see only the outward shape. What I am forming lies within. I am interested only in what remains after the pot has been broken." The potter shapes not just a vessel from the clay but also the totality of her person.[7] We give outside of ourselves in order to receive something within ourselves.

The main character in John Updike's "The Music School" begins to reflect on his life as he waits for his piano lesson. In his reverie he mingles reflections from the prior night's church discussion group with the piano lesson. "Each moment I live, I must think where to place my fingers, and press them down with no confidence of hearing a chord . . . The world is the host; it must be chewed."[8] Because we have forgotten how to press our fingers into the soil—to feel truth not just in our minds but in our bodies—we no longer find a responsive chord in our world. The world is only the sacramental host when we chew it.

This capacity to chew life, to taste its texture, to feel it glide through our fingers is central to our identity. We experience our identity in action, or at least in the possibility for it. What happens in human experience is "I conceive—I can—I will—I am." The "I can" and the "I will" are essential to our identity.[9] To have an identity is not just to have a social security card, a mailing address, or a telephone number in a thick book. Identity is something we create for ourselves by the choices we make and by the actions we take. It is to respond to life in definite ways. Identity is our witness to truth in our lives. We are made by what we make. In this the outer and the inner converge.

Our personal identity as creators is a broken

fragment of our original status before God. We are the distorted image of a creative, generative God. In the beginning we experienced no split between mind and body. Work and thought were one. We could think with our hands. We were co-creators with God. The craving for the tree of knowledge, however, resulted in our tragic distortion. Knowledge, the life of the mind, became more important than the totality of our doing and being. Work that was meant as a blessing became a curse. Adam and Eve must gain their bread by the sweat of their brow (Gen. 3:17-19). Yet because work is nonetheless a fragment of our original divine image, it also is the link that connects us to our Creator. Our Creator gave us the possibility of reenacting God's own creative work in our small, humble tasks. Generativity characterizes both God and humanity. We alone among the species have the capacity to envision a future and then to create it. We consciously choose how we will create and how we will respond to what we have generated.

Don Mitchell's fable, *The Souls of Lambs*, tells of a shepherd who reflects on the meaning of his life as he tends his sheep through one year. He watches a ram and a ewe sport and breed in the tupping pasture. He carefully guides his sheep through the birthing process. He even sleeps in the barn to be near them should they need his help in birthing their lambs. He saves the tender second cutting of hay for the young lambs. He weans them and finally slaughters a young lamb with his own hands and eats it.

As the narrator fries and eats his firstborn lamb, he reflects upon the meaning of what he has seen and done. Mitchell's categories seem slightly dated to us and their language is that of an era not as sensitive to sexist language as our own is. The language and the wisdom are drawn from the ancient pool of folk wisdom that those engaged in menial labor have preserved over the centuries. Intellectual fashions come and go. Folk wisdom endures.

The shepherd, Mitchell observes, can sense three modes of loving. There is the raw passion of the ram and the ewe in the tupping pasture. This passion has its limits. It cannot care for what it creates. The ram that conceives life in the pasture is not concerned about the lamb he fathers. Passion generates life but does not tend it. The second mode of loving is motherhood. The ewe loves her lambs. Sometimes she loves them too much. Her love preserves them in life and protects them. This is its strength; but it also is imperfect. It makes an excess of loving. It knows how to hold on to life but not how to let go. It lacks trust in its creations. It cannot release its lambs into the larger world. The third mode of loving is animal husbandry. This is the care provided by the shepherd. It combines a passionate love for the animals with a necessary capacity to detach oneself from them. It knows both when to enfold and when to release. Even this mode of loving is imperfect. In fact, it is the weakest of the three. The other two are grounded in instinct. The ram does not choose to mate with the ewe because of love. The ewe does not decide to suckle her lambs. The shepherd, on the other hand, must decide to care for the sheep. The shepherd must both choose to create and decide to let go.[10]

This imperfect capacity to create and to care is both our human strength and our great weakness. God made us in the divine image in order that we might be generative: to create and to care, to love and to work. This generative capacity is no longer grounded in our instincts. We must decide to love and to work. Like Mitchell's shepherd, our generative capacity issues from our human freedom.

This is also the potter's concern. How can I ensure that passion and involvement will be made luminous without being cooled? How can the inner fire that consumes be transfigured into the light that illuminates? The potter must turn the inner vision of ideas into an outer reality. The truth of an insight is not truth until it is felt in the body and in the clay. Mitchell's shepherd must know how to turn his haphazard passions into deliberate compassion. Is this not also the goal of Christian transformation?

In the Coptic life of St. Pachomius, we read how early in his life Pachomius and his brother were praying to know God's will for them. They were living in an abandoned village, Tabbenese, and earned their bread by helping the neighboring farmers with their harvest. One night, after their common prayer, Pachomius goes apart to seek God's will. A luminous figure appears and asks, "Why are you desolate and brokenhearted?"

"Because I seek the will of God," replies Pachomius.

The figure tells him: "It is the will of God that you serve the human race, in order to reconcile it with God."

Pachomius cannot believe what he has been told. "I ask about the will of God and you tell me to serve my brothers and sisters?"

The angel can only reply: "It is God's will that you serve men and women in order to bring them to God."[11]

There is also a Zen story about a pious woman who built a hermitage for a monk and for years maintained his hermitage and fed him. Finally she decided to test his authenticity. She sent her pretty niece with his food and told her to embrace the monk and then tell her how he reacted to this advance. When the niece embraced the monk, he roughly pushed her away, saying, "Sap does not rise in a withered tree!" The niece returned to her aunt and reported the incident. In a fit of anger the pious woman stormed up to the hermitage and drove away the monk and burned the hermitage. "For years I have been looking after a block of wood," she cried. The woman felt that the monk's religious devotions had turned him into a block of wood, something with no feeling, no sensitivity, and no emotion. His religion had deadened him to experience. Our attempts at spiritual formation are false when they crush our tenderness and compassion, our care and generativity.[12]

Our lives are meant to image the divine Creator whose mode of loving is that of creation and redemption, work and love. These qualities are those of the shepherd. They are the marks of faithful Christian living.

> What does it profit, my brethren, if a man says he has faith but has not works? Can his faith save him? If a brother or sister is ill-clad and in lack of daily food, and one of you says to them, "Go in peace, be warmed and filled," without giving them the things needed for the body, what does it profit? So faith by itself, if it has no works, is dead. . . . For as the body apart from the spirit is dead, so faith apart from works is dead.
> —James 2:14-17, 26

Gwendolen Greene, in her introduction to Baron von Hugel's letters, recalls how he once told her in a letter: "Christianity has taught us to care. Caring is the greatest thing—caring matters most. My faith is not enough—it comes and goes."[13]

Pottery reminds us that our redemption comes not when we ponder deep thoughts or when we have wonderful experiences. Creation and redemption are two sides of the same coin, and both are of the body.

When we can identify with our Creator's capacity to create and to care, then our salvation is near. It comes in the concrete deed, in the act of compassion, in the care of bodies and the care of souls. Whoever has been renewed according to the image of Christ can no longer see God without seeing the world or the world without seeing God.

Notes

Introduction
1. Adelaide A. Pollard, "Have Thine Own Way, Lord," *The Methodist Hymnal* (Nashville: The Methodist Publishing House, 1966), no. 154.

Chapter 1. Gathering the Raw Materials
1. Rivka Gonen, *Ancient Pottery* (London: Cassells Publishing, 1973), p. 9.
2. Gonen, pp. 10-11.
3. Lyall Watson, *Lifetide* (New York: Bantam Books, 1980), p. 93.
4. Lewis Thomas, *The Lives of a Cell* (New York: Bantam Books, 1975), p. 2.
5. Lewis Thomas, *The Medusa and the Snail* (New York: Bantam Books, 1980), p. 23.
6. Erik Erikson, *Insight and Responsibility* (New York: W. W. Norton and Company, Inc., 1964), p. 87.

Chapter 2. Wedging the Raw Clay
1. Friedrich von Hugel, *Letters from Baron Friedrich von Hugel to a Niece*, ed. Gwendolen Greene (London: J. M. Dent and Sons, Ltd., 1929), p 25.
2. Watson, p. 50.
3. Thomas, *The Lives of a Cell*, pp. 3-4.
4. Lawrence Kushner, *The River of Light* (San Francisco: Harper and Row, Publishers, 1981), p. 78.
5. John Donne, "Meditation xvii, Devotions upon Emergent

Occasions," *Norton Anthology of English Literature* (New York: W. W. Norton and Company, Inc., 1962), vol. 1, p. 917.

6. Gerard Manley Hopkins, *The Poems of Gerard Manley Hopkins*, eds. W. H. Gardner and N. H. MacKenzie (London: Oxford University Press, 1970), p. 88.

7. Charles Williams, *Descent into Hell* (Grand Rapids, MI: William B. Eerdmans Publishing Company, 1949), p. 99.

8. Williams, p. 188.

9. James Weldon Johnson, *God's Trombones* (New York: The Viking Press, 1969), pp. 17-20.

10. Douglas Steere, *Dimensions of Prayer* (New York: Women's Division, Board of Global Ministries, United Methodist Church, 1962), p. 18.

11. Charles Hartshorne, *A Natural Theology for our Time* (La Salle, IL: Open Court, 1973), p. 101.

12. William Reiser, *The Potter's Touch* (New York: Paulist Press, 1981), p. 10.

Chapter 3. Opening Up the Center

1. Evelyn Underhill, *The Spiritual Life* (New York: Harper and Row, Publishers, no date), p. 74.

2. Rainer Maria Rilke, *Letters to a Young Poet*, trans., M. D. Herter Norton (New York: W. W. Norton and Company, Inc., 1962), p. 64.

3. Dietrich Bonhoeffer, *Creation and Fall: Temptation*, trans., J. C. Fletcher and K. Downham (New York: The Macmillan Company, 1966), p. 53.

4. Pierre Teilhard de Chardin, *The Divine Milieu* (New York: Harper and Row, Publishers, 1965), pp. 92-93.

5. Simone Weil, *Waiting for God*, trans., E. Craufurd (New York: Harper Colophon Books, 1973), p. 106.

6. Weil, p. 115.

7. Dionysius the Areopagite, *The Divine Names and the Mystical Theology*, trans., C. E. Rolt (London: SPCK, 1979), pp. 137-38.

8. Matthew the Poor, *The Communion of Love* (Crestwood, NY: St. Vladimir's Seminary Press, 1984), p. 218.

9. Thomas Merton, *Contemplation in a World of Action* (Garden City, NY: Image Books, 1973), p. 141.

10. John Milton, *Paradise Lost* (London: Longman House, 1971), pp. 637-38.

11. Reinhold Niebuhr, *The Nature and Destiny of Man* (New York: Charles Scribner's Sons, 1943), vol. 1, p. 260.

Chapter 4. Throwing the Pot

1. Bonhoeffer, *Creation and Fall: Temptation*, pp. 66-67.
2. Bonhoeffer, *Creation and Fall: Temptation*, p. 73.
3. Milton, pp. 497-98.
4. Dietrich Bonhoeffer, *The Cost of Discipleship* (London: SCM Press Ltd., 1964), p. 270.
5. Ernest Becker, *The Denial of Death* (New York: The Free Press, 1973), p. 107.
6. Becker, p. 170.
7. Stanley Milgram, *Obedience to Authority* (New York: Harper and Row, Publishers, 1974), pp. 133-34.
8. Leander Keck, *Paul and His Letters* (Philadelphia: Fortress Press, 1979), p. 52.

Chapter 5. Firing the Bisque Ware

1. Gaston Bachelard, *The Psychoanalysis of Fire*, trans., A.C.M. Ross (Boston: Beacon Press, 1968), p. 25.
2. Bachelard, p. 16.
3. Bachelard, p. 7.
4. Kushner, p. 91.
5. Richard Rolle, *The Fire of Love and the Mending of Life*, trans., M. L. del Mastro (Garden City, NY: Image Books, 1981), p. 93.
6. Rolle, p. 106.
7. T. S. Eliot, *The Complete Poems and Plays 1909-1950* (New York: Harcourt Brace Jovanovich, 1971), pp. 143-44.
8. Søren Kierkegaard, *Purity of Heart*, trans., Douglas Steere (New York: Harper and Row, Publishers, 1956), p. 218.
9. Paul S. Minear, *Images of the Church in the New Testament* (Philadelphia: The Westminster Press, 1960), pp. 52-56.
10. Rollo May, *Love and Will* (New York: Dell Publishing Co., Inc., 1969), p. 205.
11. Sister Carol Marie Wildt, "The Role of the Imagination in the Ministry of Spiritual Formation," unpublished paper, pp. 10-16.
12. May, p. 223.
13. Charles Wesley, "Jesus, Thine All-Victorious Love," *The Methodist Hymnal* (Nashville: The Methodist Publishing House, 1966), no. 278.
14. Bonhoeffer, *The Cost of Discipleship*, p. 201.
15. David J. Hassel, *Radical Prayer* (New York: Paulist Press, 1983), p. 46.
16. William Johnston, *The Mirror Mind* (San Francisco: Harper and Row, Publishers, 1981), p. 92.

17. St. Augustine, *The Confessions*, trans., J. M. Lelen (New York: Catholic Book Publishing Co., 1952), p. 199.

18. Matthew the Poor, p. 37.

19. Raymond E. Brown, *The Gospel According to John I-XII* (Garden City, NY: Doubleday and Company, Inc., 1966), pp. 230-304.

20. Dom Gregory Dix, *The Shape of the Liturgy* (London: Dacre Press, 1970), pp. 243-46.

21. Johnston, pp. 66-67.

22. von Hugel, p. 46.

Chapter 6. Applying the Glaze

1. Erik Erikson, *Childhood and Society* (New York: W. W. Norton and Company, Inc., 1963), p. 250.

2. C. G. Jung, *Modern Man in Search of a Soul*, trans., W. S. Dell and C. F. Baynes (New York: Harcourt Brace Jovanovich, 1933), p. 229.

3. Augustine, p. 21.

4. Par Lagerkvist, *Barabbas* (New York: Bantam Books, 1962), p. 99.

5. Pierre Teilhard de Chardin, *Hymn of the Universe*, (New York: Harper and Row, Publishers, 1972), p. 138.

6. Teilhard de Chardin, *Hymn of the Universe*, p. 139.

7. Anthony de Mello, *The Song of the Bird* (Anand, India: Gujarat Sahitya Prakash, 1982), pp. 18-19.

8. Christopher Fry, "The Firstborn," Religious Drama, 1 (New York: Meridian Books, 1957), p. 88.

Chapter 7. Evaluating the Finished Product

1. Alexander Pope, "An Essay on Man," *Complete Poetical Works* (Boston: Houghton Mifflin Company, 1931), p. 139.

2. Fry, p. 120.

3. *The Book of Worship* (Nashville: The Methodist Publishing House, 1965), p. 387.

4. Jean-Pierre de Caussade, *Abandonment to Divine Providence*, trans., John Beevers (Garden City, NY: Image Books, 1975), p. 79.

5. Hannah Whitall Smith, *The Christian's Secret of a Happy Life*, (New York: Fleming H. Revell Company, 1888), p. 196.

6. Eliot, p. 134.

Chapter 8. Caring for the Creation

1. Gonen, p. 14.

2. Thomas Hardy, *The Complete Poems of Thomas Hardy* (New York: Macmillan Publishing Co., 1976), p. 543.

3. de Caussade, p. 39.

4. William Shakespeare, *The Sonnets* (New York: Avenel Books, 1961), p. 81.

5. Richard Jeffries, *Landscape with Figures: an Anthology,* ed., Richard Mabey (New York: Penguin Books, 1983), p. 57.

6. Wendell Berry, *The Unsettling of America* (New York: Avon Books, 1977), p. 140.

7. Mary C. Richards, *Centering in Pottery, Poetry and the Person* (Middletown, CT: Wesleyan University Press, 1964), p. 13.

8. John Updike, "The Music School," *The Music School* (New York: Fawcett Crest Books, 1967), p. 143.

9. May, pp. 241-42.

10. Don Mitchell, *The Souls of Lambs* (Boston: Houghton Mifflin Company, 1979), pp. 103-105.

11. Merton, 287-88.

12. Johnston, p. 113.

13. von Hugel, p. xliii.

About the Author

Thomas R. Hawkins is pastor of Hope United Methodist Church in Belchertown, Massachusetts. He received the B.A. degree from Eastern Illinois University, the M.A. degree from Indiana University and from Harvard University, and the M. Div. degree from Christian Theological Seminary in Indianapolis.

Mr. Hawkins has been a participant in The Upper Room's Academy for Spiritual Formation, and he is the spiritual director of the Southern New England Walk to Emmaus. He is the author of *The Unsuspected Power of the Psalms*.

In addition to his interest in pottery, Mr. Hawkins plays the flute.